A Parent's & Teacher's Handbook on Identifying and Preventing
Child Abuse

eleone
arent
ook or
iting

GWM

G.W. Medical Publishing, Inc.
St. Louis, Missouri 1998

The G.W. Medical Publishing Mission

———— ♦ ————

To become the world leader in publishing and information services

on child abuse, maltreatment and diseases, and domestic violence.

We seek to heighten awareness of these issues and provide relevant

information to professionals and consumers.

A portion of our profits is contributed to non-profit
organizations dedicated to the prevention of child abuse
and the care of victims of abuse and other children
and family charities.

A Parent's & Teacher's Handbook on
Identifying and Preventing

Child Abuse

JAMES A. MONTELEONE, M.D.

Professor of Pediatrics and Gynecology
Saint Louis University School of Medicine
Director of the Division of Child Protection
Cardinal Glennon Children's Hospital
St. Louis, Missouri

GWM

G.W. Medical Publishing, Inc.
St. Louis, Missouri 1998

Publisher: Marianne and Glenn Whaley

Design Director: Glenn Whaley

Developmental Editor: Elaine Steinborn

Editor: Mary Brockgreitens

Production Manager: William R. Anderson
  –Book Design/Page Layout: Sue E. White
  –Cover Design: Dee Ann Lange; Sue E. White
  –Production: GW Graphics

Indexer: Linda Caravelli

Printed in the United States of America

G. W. Medical Publishing, Inc.
2601 Metro Blvd., St. Louis, Missouri 63043
Phone: 314-298-0330; fax: 314-298-2820
info@gwmedical.com
www.gwmedical.com

Library of Congress Cataloging-in-Publication Data
Monteleone, James A.
  A parent's & teacher's handbook on identifying and preventing
child abuse / James A. Monteleone.
        p.   cm.
  Includes bibliographical references and index.
  ISBN 1-878060-27-9 (pbk. : alk. paper)
  1. Child abuse—United States. 2. Abused children—United States—
Identification. 3. Child abuse—United States—Prevention.
I. Title.
HV6626.52.M66   1998
363.2′595554—dc21   98-22804
                                                          CIP

ISBN 1-878060-27-9

CONTRIBUTORS

Karen M. Bly, R.N., B.S.N., M.A., M. Ed.
Nurse/Counselor
Child Protection Unit
Cardinal Glennon Children's Hospital
St. Louis, Missouri

Detective Joe Bova Conti
Child Abuse Investigator
Maryland Heights Police Department
Maryland Heights, Missouri

Theodore A. Henderson, M.D., Ph.D.

Vicki McNeese, M.S.
Staff Psychologist
Cardinal Glennon Children's Hospital
Adjunct Instructor of Psychology
Saint Louis University
St. Louis, Missouri

James A. Monteleone, M.D.
Professor of Pediatrics and Gynecology
Saint Louis University School of Medicine
Director of the Division of Child Protection
Cardinal Glennon Children's Hospital
St. Louis, Missouri

Wayne I. Munkel, M.S.W., L.C.S.W.
Supervisor of Social Services
Cardinal Glennon Children's Hospital
Lecturer, School of Social Work
University of Missouri—St. Louis
St. Louis, Missouri

Jay E. Noffsinger, M.D.
Professor of Pediatrics
Saint Louis University School of Medicine
Cardinal Glennon Children's Hospital

Peggy S. Pearl, Ed.D.
Professor, Department of Consumer and Family
Studies
Southwest Missouri State University
Springfield, Missouri

Becky J. Powers
United States Postal Inspector

Colette M. Rickert, M.A.T., L.P.C.C., A.T.R.-BC
American Art Therapy Association
American Counseling Association

Scott Skinner
Agent
Federal Bureau of Investigation
Washington, D.C.

Allan F. Stewart
Attorney
Beach, Burcke, Helfers, Mittleman and Stewart, L.L.C.
St. Louis, Missouri

Detective Michael Sullivan
Internet Crimes Unit
Naperville Police Department
Naperville, Illinois

Foreword by:
Howard B. Levy, M.D.
Chair, Department of Pediatrics;
Director, Pediatric Ecology Program,
Columbia Grant Hospital;
President, International Society for the
Prevention of Child Abuse and Neglect

With special contributions by:
Joan Boyer
Jon Boyer
M. Susan Clements
Stacey Ann Lannert
Deb Underwood

TO PATTY, PATRICK, LISA, GABRIEL AND DACEY

FOREWORD

This book is written for parents and professionals who want to help parents deal with the complex and confusing issues that surround child abuse. Although the phenomenon of child abuse is neither new nor at an epidemic level, parents who are raising children in today's world are faced with a seemingly endless number of challenges that never faced previous generations. Changes in the basic family structure and values combined with diminished support systems can easily make child rearing appear to be a frightening and formidable task.

Over the past forty-plus years, several books have been published to help parents raise happy and healthy children. From my perspective, two of these publications have been pivotal in offering the information needed to develop the basic foundation so necessary to child rearing. Dr. Benjamin Spock's first book, *Baby and Child Care,* provided past generations of caretakers with a comprehensive guide for raising children. More than twenty years later, in 1987, Marilyn Heins and Anne Seiden published *Child Care-Parent Care, A Comprehensive Sourcebook of Medical, Practical and Commonsense Advice on Caring for Your Children during the Parenting Years.* Despite the more recent focus by the media on child abuse and the accompanying explosion of written and online material on this subject, there is still a paucity of information available to lessen the confusion and anxiety of parents seeking to understand the complex topic of child abuse.

Dr. Monteleone's timely publication, *A Parent's & Teacher's Handbook on Identifying and Preventing Child Abuse,* meets the need. Beginning with its eye-catching cover, this book is written expressly to respond to the concerns of parents and teachers. Dr. Monteleone and his co-authors seek to ease the fears and address the needs of parents, who often feel helpless to protect their children in a seemingly hostile environment. Each author approaches his or her topic with professionalism and sensitivity to the needs of caretakers. They have been successful in producing a practical and almost exhaustive resource for parents. Furthermore, they have brought reason and logic to a topic with which parents are often assailed. The content is provided in a straightforward manner using terms that are aimed at the lay person rather than the clinician. Although parents are the intended audience, the detail and broad scope covered provide a welcome addition to the existing technical and scientific material available to professionals in the field of child abuse.

The chapter on behavioral indicators is particularly well written and offers the reader a comprehensive overview of the subject. The author is careful to emphasize that changes in a child's behavior must not be interpreted as indicating child abuse, but rather serve as a stimulus to seek professional evaluation. Care is taken to explain that an indicator is not a litmus test but rather a signal to attract attention. The importance of understanding that, while behavioral changes may result from abuse, they may just as likely be caused by other stresses faced by the child, is well explained. This chapter is also noteworthy because it provides essential information without causing undue alarm. Furthermore, the chapter clearly indicates exactly what steps parents should take after behavioral indicators of abuse are identified.

Little needs to be said about the chapter on physical indicators of abuse written by Dr. Monteleone. This chapter is written with the same thoroughness and ease of readability that characterized the author's two-volume professional textbook on child abuse. Indicators of physical abuse are well illustrated by specific examples and illustrations. Parents reading this chapter should be fully equipped to understand what physical abuse looks like and what to do if it is found in their child.

This book is essential reading for parents and teachers seeking to understand child abuse and for others who are likely to come into contact with abused children or concerned parents. The information presented is practical, pragmatic, and eminently usable. *A Parent's & Teacher's Handbook on Identifying and Preventing Child Abuse* may provide for parents seeking to learn about child abuse what Dr. Spock's *Baby and Child Care* and Drs. Heins and Seiden's *Child Care-Parent Care* provided to parents desiring practical and commonsense advice on caring for children.

Howard B. Levy, M.D.
Chair, Department of Pediatrics;
Director, Pediatric Ecology Program,
Columbia Grant Hospital;
President, International Society for the
Prevention of Child Abuse and Neglect

PREFACE

I had barely started celebrating the completion of the second edition of the *Child Maltreatment* two-volume set when I was approached to write this book for parents. Based on their response to the publisher's website, it was clear that parents were searching for practical information on child abuse and nothing was meeting their need. I've dealt with child abuse cases for years in the hospital emergency room and in death investigations, and it was exciting to put together a book to address the "front line" of this important social problem.

In planning the book I tried to remember the many questions parents and colleagues have asked over the years in the hospital, at conferences and during investigations. Among them are:

- **What is child abuse?** You'll see what it is, what it isn't, and the important physical and behavioral indicators parents can look for in their children. I've tried to use illustrations to show as well as tell about the injuries and conduct abuse produces.

- **How do I talk to my child about sexual abuse?** Talking to your child and making him or her comfortable enough to share with you are essential–and the information offered on how to communicate with children is practical to the nth degree. You will be fully equipped to address any body safety issues and able to empower your child in all situations.

- **Who are these abusers? Are my children at risk?** You'll find the characteristics to look for in child care providers and be alerted to situations that can facilitate abuse. Plus you'll see what to do to avoid the danger and keep your child safe in school, on the playground, in your home with a babysitter, or while participating in sports or other youth activities.

- **How do I cope if my child is abused?** Not only do you get the step-by-step information you need about these situations, but you will read the words of abused children and their mothers as they are recovering from abusive encounters. This book outlines how to react to your child's disclosure, what to expect from the legal system, and how art therapy can be used to help in the discovery and treatment phases of abuse.

As you can tell, more than anything else, I wanted this book to be practical and give parents a hands-on, bottom-line, everyday guide to what child abuse is and what they can do about it. In each chapter information is organized in an easy-to-retrieve format with many highlighted lists, tables, and boxes, direct instructions, and summary points. The illustrations were chosen very carefully to help readers clearly identify abusive or neglectful situations.

The contributors to this effort represent all of the areas that are touched by child abuse—emergency room physicians, teachers, therapists, social workers, and abused children themselves. Thanks to all of them for working on these chapters in the midst of all their other commitments. These are truly caring individuals. A special expression of gratitude goes to the parents of abused children and the abused children, now adults, who shared their personal stories in Chapters 10 and 11. I know that this was both painful and healing for them.

Thanks also to Glenn Whaley and his staff, who developed the initial plan for the book and with whom I worked closely to bring it all together. And finally, thanks to my editor, Elaine Steinborn. I have appreciated her expertise in editing my professional publications, but I was equally impressed with the way she shaped and reworked this manuscript into a very readable, parent-friendly style.

This book is dedicated both to children and to the parents who love them and want to care for them to the best of their ability. It is my hope that someday no child will be exposed to abuse or neglect of any kind. This book is offered as a tool to use in building a society that truly cares about its children.

James A. Monteleone
May 8, 1998

TABLE OF CONTENTS

CHAPTER 4   JAMES A. MONTELEONE
SEXUAL ABUSE 45

CHAPTER 5   WAYNE I. MUNKEL
NEGLECT AND ABANDONMENT 55

CHAPTER 10   JON BOYER, STACEY ANN LANNERT, AND M. SUSAN CLEMENTS

TALES OF THREE INCEST SURVIVORS

CHAPTER 11   JOAN BOYER AND DEB UNDERWOOD

PARENTS WHOSE CHILDREN WERE ABUSED

CHAPTER 12   COLETTE M. RICKERT

ART THERAPY

CHAPTER 13   PEGGY S. PEARL

PREVENTION OF ABUSE

CHAPTER 14   MICHAEL SULLIVAN, JOE BOVA CONTI, BECKY J. POWERS AND SCOTT SKINNER

REVIEWS

"I've had 30-plus years of experience working with families on child care issues and I've not seen any reference which covers as wide a range of information as this book does. It definitely fills a gap in the literature.

"Parenting styles and discipline are topics parents are eager to learn about. Linking these topics to the potential for child abuse, as this book does, helps to prevent the abuse from happening.

"I also found the chapter on how to talk to your kids about personal safety issues to be impressive and invaluable. This is a disturbing subject which none of us wishes to think about or, lacking the right words, talk about. But we have to empower our kids. This book gives parents the right words to use which are not scary and are put in the context of all other parts of development."

Kaye Levy
Coordinator, Better Beginnings Grant;
Teacher/Trainer, Montessori Method,
Gloucester, VA

"After reviewing the handbook, which your office provided me, I believe this book will be a valuable asset for parents and teachers who are trying to prevent child abuse. The discussion is straightforward, factual and easy to understand. The checklists in the book will enable the parent to make intelligent choices about selecting childcare givers and facilities. The discussion of the warning signs for child abuse gives lay persons insight when talking to their children and the ability to understand not only what is said but the body language of these young people.

"I wish you nothing but the best success in promoting the handbook, which should become a standard by which other child abuse guides are measured."

Frank A. Conard
Administrative Judge of the Family Court
Eleventh Judicial Circuit, Division Four
St. Charles, Missouri

"Karen Bly and Jim Monteleone's compassion and commitment to children victimized by sexual abuse is evidenced not only in their clinical work, but in this very helpful and understandable book. Parents and teachers alike will not be able to escape the usefulness of this excellent text. This will be a book I will recommend and hope to implement in our program's educational programs."

Julie Maire-Turner, M.Ed.
Executive Director
Children's Advocacy Center of St. Louis

A Parent's & Teacher's Handbook on Identifying and Preventing
Child Abuse

In 1995, a case of child abuse was reported in the United States every 10 seconds.

Source: *Current Trends in Child Abuse Reporting and Fatalities: The Results of the 1995 Annual Fifty State Survey*, National Center on Child Abuse Prevention Research.

PRINCIPLES OF DISCIPLINE: WHAT IS AND IS NOT ABUSE

Jay E. Noffsinger, M.D.

Volumes have been written on how to be an effective parent and how to discipline children. This chapter focuses on some general principles of behavior modification that can potentially decrease the likelihood that children will be physically abused. The topics covered are:

- *Parenting styles––what works and what doesn't*
- *Positive reinforcement––how to use it*
- *Negative reinforcement––administering punishment*
- *Expectations and rules––reality check*
- *Physical punishment––when it is appropriate and guidelines for its use*

PARENTING STYLES—WHAT WORKS AND WHAT DOESN'T

What constitutes "effective parenting?" A parental response that is appropriate for one child in a certain situation may be very inappropriate or ineffective for another child or situation. Because we live in a "results-oriented" society, perhaps we can agree on this concept:

We have basically succeeded as parents if our children make it to adulthood feeling very good about themselves as individuals and continuing to both love and respect us as their parents.

While much could be added to this statement, it provides a framework for exploring methods of behavior modification that are likely to produce this result.

Let me give you some examples of parenting styles.

Joan and Michael Smith are very well intentioned. They have heard from others that it is important to be strict so as not to lose control of their children. Of course, they expect their children to behave and follow the rules. When the children obey, they don't really receive any special recognition, since they are just meeting expectations. However, when the children break rules or misbehave, they are always noticed and punished.

What are the results of this parenting style? Generally the home atmosphere is very negative. For example, on one occasion, Michael lost control when he was punishing his 8-year-old son just because he was angry. He slapped the boy on the face, leaving obvious marks. Afterward, he felt terrible because he had been unable to control his emotions.

Children who are subjected to the style chosen by this family may well grow up with low self-esteem and in fear of their parents. They tend to be extremely unwilling to bring problems to their parents' attention. These children may even rebel against this authority and choose to behave in ways that are potentially dangerous. Finally, and even more unfortunately, the children may eventually become parents who use the same parenting style and thus repeat the same harmful mistakes.

Here's another example:

In the Jones family, Maria and Tom also have rules. They talked about the rules with their children to be sure that everyone understood what they were. They are very consistent in noticing when rules have been broken and in administering punishment when needed. However, they spend most of their time trying to catch their children being good. When they spot good behavior, they immediately praise that specific behavior and make sure the child knows how good his or her behavior makes them feel as parents.

What is the result? The atmosphere in this home is generally positive, while the children still learn to respect the "rules of the house." These children are likely to grow up feeling very good about themselves as individuals and to continue to love and respect their parents.

Which of These Parenting Styles Makes More Sense?

Children are likely to end up feeling good about themselves as adults if they have been raised in a very positive environment. The hallmarks of a positive environment are:

- Children are consistently and frequently recognized and rewarded for doing what is right.

- Children are also consistently and frequently recognized and rewarded for working very hard at something——even if their efforts are ultimately unsuccessful.

> "A general principle of behavior modification is that behaviors we want to persist should be positively rewarded."

As parents, we all need to try harder to "catch our children being good" so we can recognize this good behavior. But it's not easy because it goes against human nature. We expect our children to be good, so when they are good we tend to take the good behavior for granted. When we see bad behavior, on the other hand, we always seem to reward it in a negative way. This has been called the ***criticism trap.***

A general principle of behavior modification is that behaviors we want to persist should be positively rewarded.

- At the beginning of each day, adopt the attitude that you are going to watch your child and give an immediate reward when you "catch" your child being good.

- At the end of each day, review any opportunities you may have missed for catching your child being good so you can do better the next day.

Applying this principle effectively takes a lot of practice because it doesn't come naturally. We just don't feel compelled to reward effort and improvement in skills rather than just success. Do your children participate in sports and physical activity? Nearly 75% of children 5 to 6 years old participate in team sports because they have fun. Yet only about 20% of high school students continue to be actively involved. The other 55% drop out because *the activity is no longer fun.* Why has it ceased to be fun? Because adults emphasize winning and reward success rather than simply rewarding effort and improvement. If we want our children to end up as adults who have a lifelong interest in remaining physically active, we must make participation in sports fun *throughout* childhood. Children will feel good about themselves if they are praised and rewarded for trying and improving instead of being subjected to criticism for anything other than perfection. When they feel successful, children will continue to enjoy the activity. As our children participate in team sports, we should seek coaches who understand and follow this philosophy.

POSITIVE REINFORCEMENT——HOW TO USE IT

Human beings love being noticed in positive ways. When we are rewarded or recognized for good behavior, we usually try even harder to do even better so we can be praised again. This is an example of the power of positive reinforcement. When we feel good about ourselves, we have more energy and work harder to accomplish our goals.

Guidelines for Positive Reinforcement

- **Recognize good behavior as soon as you notice it—don't delay.**

- **Praise the good behavior, not the whole child.** Statements like "you are an angel" could be classified as a "warm fuzzy," which may help self-esteem, but saying such things does little to specifically modify behavior. Be specific about what behavior earned the reward or praise.

- **Make the praise descriptive rather than using judgmental terms.** For example, "Mary, it really pleases me to see you playing and sharing with your sister" would be a clear description of the behavior you want to encourage. It isn't necessary to attempt to judge *why* Mary is sharing with her sister.

> ## Guidelines for Positive Reinforcement, *con't.*
>
> - **When you are trying to encourage a certain behavior, offer short-term, intermediate, and long-term rewards.**
>
>   For example, Marty was having trouble remembering to keep his room picked up. His mom sat down with him and talked about the problem. They agreed on a mutual goal—having his room stay neat. To help encourage his good behavior, they decided that each evening his mom found the room neat at bedtime, she would read an extra story to him. They would keep track of successful days using a star on a calendar. If Marty received seven stars, he would be rewarded with a trip to the zoo. If the room stayed neat for a month, he would get a special Nintendo game he had been wanting. All of these rewards would be accompanied by lots of praise and encouragement. Some parents may object to this plan because they feel that it represents bribery. When conditions are set up beforehand, as in this example, it is not bribery but rather a great example of behavior modification by positive reinforcement. Compare this approach to the alternative—daily nagging and fighting about the room that remains dirty. This would be an example of the criticism trap we talked about.

NEGATIVE REINFORCEMENT—ADMINISTERING PUNISHMENT

Up to this point, we have been discussing positive reinforcement, which serves to strengthen desired behavior. *Negative reinforcement* (or *punishment*) tends to weaken behavior, but it is not nearly as effective in changing behavior as positive reinforcement. It can also have other undesired results. **It is always better to use positive reinforcement to shape behavior and work toward our long-term goal of raising a child who develops strong self-esteem.** If this whole book were on principles of discipline, there would be ten chapters on positive reinforcement and only one dealing with punishment.

Negative reinforcement includes both punishment and the withdrawal of positive reinforcement. Here are some general principles regarding punishment:

> ## Principles of Negative Reinforcement
>
> - **Be consistent in applying the rules that result in punishment.** This consistency applies both from one day to the next and between both parents.

Principles of Negative Reinforcement, *con't.*

- **Administer punishment in a calm, matter-of-fact way.** One of the biggest problems with physical punishment is that it is usually delivered in anger. Not only does this increase the likelihood that the parent may lose control and cross the line into physical abuse, but it teaches the child to fear and therefore avoid the parent. It also shows the child that physical aggression is an appropriate response to anger. Behaviors such as lying, cheating, sneaking, and hiding may be inadvertently encouraged when they are used to avoid being caught and punished.

- **Make it clear that** *the behavior* **is what caused the punishment or criticism, not** *the individual as a person.* The child is good; what he or she did was bad. Comments such as "you're worthless" are not only untrue, but they can irreparably damage the parent-child relationship as well as the child's self-esteem.

- **When punishment is needed, deliver it as soon as possible after the behavior that prompted it.**

- **When punishment consists of withdrawing privileges, provide clear instructions as to how the privileges can be regained. In addition, reinforce other constructive behaviors.**

EXPECTATIONS AND RULES--REALITY CHECK

We must have realistic expectations of our children when we make rules. Among the most important considerations for parents in determining expectations are the age and developmental stage of the infant or child. Infants cry for many reasons—they are hungry, they are in pain, they need to be changed, they are angry, they want love. They do not just cry to irritate us, although this is often the effect crying produces. Other annoyances also occur: infants make messes at mealtime, children have toileting accidents—the list could go on and on. Many serious episodes of physical child abuse have occurred when parents lost control in reacting to their child's natural and expected behavior. "He just would not stop crying," said the sobbing father to the paramedics who were trying to resuscitate the infant he had just shaken. You must be able to step back from situations where you feel yourself losing control before something happens you will later deeply regret. When you feel yourself losing focus and responding under the control of your emotions, simply move away from the child, perhaps even to another room, and take a few minutes to regain your composure. If you are dealing with an older child, you can tell him that you can't discuss the situation further right now, but need to be alone for a while.

In some instances, it may be appropriate to establish the "rules of the house" in settings such as a family meeting. Certainly, we need to at least listen to our children's point of view in setting up rules or in considering changes to rules. However, **it is not appropriate to argue with a child about the rules.** In doing this, you drop down to the child's level rather than maintaining your position as a parent. Parents rarely, if ever, win an argument with a child, who generally has more "staying power" in such an encounter. There are several outcomes to such arguments:

- The parent may lose control.

- The child learns that this is an acceptable reaction to future similar situations.

- The argument contributes to a generally negative environment, which we are trying to avoid in the family.

PHYSICAL PUNISHMENT—WHEN IT IS APPROPRIATE AND GUIDELINES FOR ITS USE

Is physical punishment ever appropriate? The American Academy of Pediatrics strongly opposes striking a child under any circumstances. But many parents adhere just as strongly to the adage, "Spare the rod, spoil the child." One situation in which physical punishment may be appropriate is where there is a concern about the child's or others' safety. Examples of this could be:

- When your child is about to touch a hot object

- When your child walks into the street

- When your child picks up a dangerous object such as a knife or gun

After making the situation safe, a firm but controlled open-handed spank of the buttocks or slap of the hand may reinforce the discussion about why the behavior was dangerous. What makes this situation different is that the physical punishment is not done in anger, but rather out of love and genuine concern for the child's safety. The child learns appropriate lessons while avoiding some of the concerns discussed earlier.

A good nonconfrontational way to prevent future dangerous behavior is to make the behavior physically impossible. You may place safety covers on electrical outlets or use only locked cabinets for dangerous items, including medications.

When does physical punishment become abuse? In the short term, any physical punishment that leaves a mark is inappropriate and abusive. Robert E. Hannemann, M.D., President of the American Academy of Pediatrics, recently noted in a letter: "No child should ever suffer physical or emotional injury under the guise of discipline."

How harmful is physical punishment? Taking a long-term view, a generally negative atmosphere where parents emphasize catching the child being bad and punishing this bad behavior physically or verbally can produce more damage than can physical harm inflicted on the child. What happens to the child subjected to such an atmosphere? He may end up as an adult who has low self-esteem, is fearful of parents, and is disrespectful of authority. Even more importantly, when he becomes a parent, he tends to repeat the same mistakes with his children.

What if you feel strongly that your child's behavior occasionally merits spanking? The following guidelines have been outlined by Barton D. Schmitt, M.D. in his book *Instructions for Pediatric Patients.**

Guidelines for Spanking

- **Hit only with an open hand and hit through clothing.** It is difficult to judge how hard you are hitting your child if you hit him or her with an object other than your hand. In addition, paddles and belts commonly cause bruises, and no child should be punished so severely that marks remain.

- **Hit only on the buttocks, legs, or hands.** Hitting a child on the face is demeaning as well as dangerous. As a rule of thumb, slapping the face is inappropriate at any age.

- **Give only one swat; that is enough to change behavior.** Hitting your child more than once may relieve your anger but it will probably not teach your child anything additional.

- **Don't spank children who are less than 1 year of age. Also, don't continue spanking as a punishment after your child is school-aged.** Spanking is inappropriate before your child has learned to walk and should be unnecessary after the age of 5 to 6 years. Use negotiation and discussion to resolve most differences with school-aged children.

- **Don't shake children.** Shaking carries a significant risk of causing blood clots on the brain (subdural hematomas), which are serious injuries.

- **Don't use physical punishment more than once each day.** The more your child is spanked, the less effect spanking will have.

- **Learn alternatives to physical discipline.** Isolating a child in a corner or bedroom for a time-out is much more civilized and effective. Learn how to use such forms of discipline.

Guidelines for Spanking, *con't.*

- **Never spank your child when you are out of control, scared, or drinking.** A few parents can't stop hitting their child once they start. They can't control their rage and need help for themselves, such as from Parents Anonymous groups. If you feel out of control, walk away from your child and never use physical punishment.

- **Don't use physical punishment for aggressive behavior, such as biting, hitting, or kicking.** Physical punishment under such circumstances teaches a child that it is all right for a bigger person to strike a smaller person. Aggressive children need to be taught restraint and self-control. They respond best to time-outs, which give them an opportunity to think about the pain they have caused.

- **Don't allow babysitters or teachers to spank your children.** Review the rules of the house with the babysitter or teacher and only allow the use of methods such as time-out to discipline your children.

* Reprinted with permission from WB Saunders Co., Philadelphia, PA, 1992.

There is no "one right way" to raise a child. There will always be controversy about what constitutes effective parenting and especially about what short-term and long-term consequences result from physical punishment. However, by applying the principles of behavior modification noted, including a heavy emphasis on positive reinforcement, we can significantly increase the likelihood that our children will turn into adults who feel good about themselves. The love and respect they develop for us as their parents will carry over to their own children and for generations to come. The importance of the choices we make as their parental role models cannot be overemphasized.

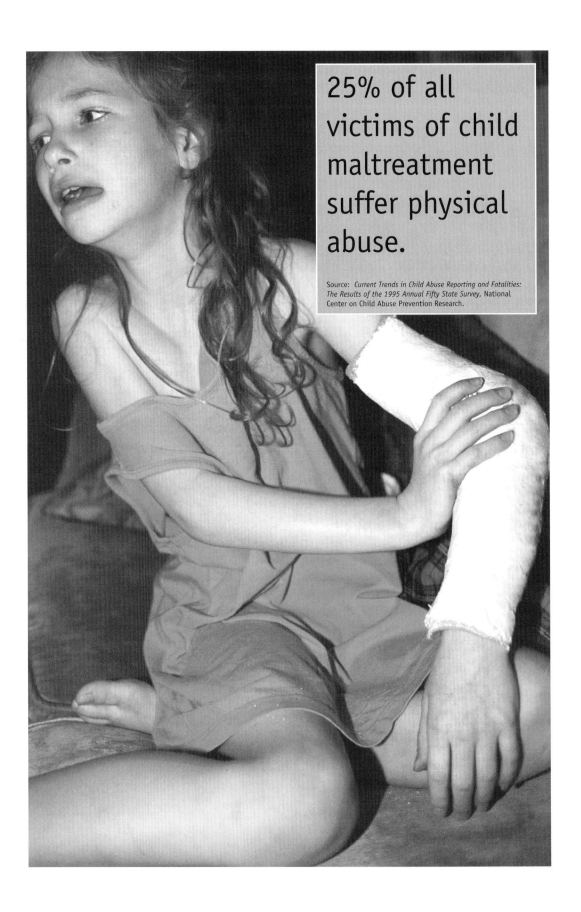

25% of all victims of child maltreatment suffer physical abuse.

Source: *Current Trends in Child Abuse Reporting and Fatalities: The Results of the 1995 Annual Fifty State Survey,* National Center on Child Abuse Prevention Research.

PHYSICAL INDICATORS OF ABUSE

JAMES A. MONTELEONE, M.D.

When your child comes home from daycare with an injury, what should you, as a parent, do? When you return home and find that your son has been injured while in the care of a babysitter, how should you respond? What would make you consider abuse rather than accepting a report of the accident from the daycare center? What signs would you see if your child was abused by a babysitter? Or, you may be a friend, neighbor, relative, or even Sunday School teacher of children. How can you tell if a child is being abused? What signs can you look for in the child's physical appearance? This chapter will look at the physical indicators of abuse, specifically:

- *Facts about injuries in children*
- *Falls in the home*
- *Skin injuries*
- *Patterns and locations of injuries*
- *Drowning*
- *Suffocation and SIDS*
- *Head injuries*
- *Burns*
- *Shaken infant syndrome*
- *Fetal abuse and neonaticide*
- *False allegations*

Child abuse is a complex problem that affects every segment of society. No social, ethnic, religious, or professional group is exempt. It can be seen as neglect or as physical, psychological, or sexual injury caused by a caretaker—whether a parent or a babysitter or a neighbor or a teacher. These injuries can result from acts of commission or acts of omission.

Legally, the term *child abuse* can refer to a range of behavior. It may be limited to intentional injury or may include any act that stunts a child's development as an individual. The definition can also consider the parents' intent, although a child is no less injured or less dead because a caretaker did not intend for the injury to occur.

We live in a violent society, and children are often the targets of that violence. Violent behavior is most likely to erupt in the home and is usually caused by a family member. People who were abused as children are more apt to become abusive parents than are those who were not abused as children. In addition, social factors, such as poverty, unemployment, and isolation, can increase the risk of child abuse.

An experienced physician can easily diagnose the classic maltreated child who has *multiple injuries in differing stages of healing;* often even a nonprofessional can see this. However, being sure that a *single injury* is inflicted can be difficult even for professional healthcare workers. Why is it important to decide whether an injury is intentional or inflicted? If a child is being abused but you decide that the injury was accidental, the child is left in the care of persons who may injure him again. In addition, other children in the situation may also be subject to abuse. On the other hand, if you feel the injury was inflicted and you are wrong, the caretakers are falsely accused and mistakenly branded as abusers.

The injuries to children are neither all abuse, nor are they all accidental. To recognize abuse you must first believe that abuse is a possibility—that the injury could have been produced intentionally. Then you can decide how to proceed.

FACTS ABOUT INJURIES IN CHILDREN

The first question you must ask yourself is, "Could this injury have occurred as the individual has described?" Then you must decide if the child is developmentally mature enough to have caused the injury. **If the caretaker tells you that the child was injured by doing something that he or she is not developmentally able to do, or if the injury is too severe to be caused by the incident described, you must decide that the history is incorrect and the injury is probably abuse.**

Children are forward moving and generally explore what is in front of them. Therefore most accidental injuries occur to the front of the

**Figure 2-1. *a,* ** *Areas where accidental injury generally occurs.*

child's body and involve the skin's surface. Often there are bruises or cuts on the forehead, nose, chin, palms, elbows, and shins **(see Plate 2-1,a)**. Here the bone is close to the surface of the skin and when the child falls or bumps into things, injuries occur.

Hand injuries can occur accidentally, such as when a child breaks a fall or when he is exploring a dangerous object, such as a hot iron. Usually these situations cause palm injuries in younger children or fingertip injuries in older children. **Injuries to the backs of hands are always suspicious, since children do not explore with the backs of their hands.** Symmetrical injuries are also very suspicious because usually the child falls to the left or right or is exploring with one hand or the other, generally not both. Remember—the hands are a common area where punishment may be inflicted. Abuse can occur when the caretaker uses excessive force or inappropriate harshness when punishing the child.

Injuries to the buttocks, genital area, abdomen, and back, as well as injuries on the sides of the body, particularly the side of the face, are often signs of abuse (see Figure 2-1,b). A bruised abdomen is highly unusual. Bruising in the genital area is generally evidence of intentional harm.

The child's age is crucial in evaluating physical injuries. Infants who can't yet walk and who are receiving good care are rarely injured. Infants who are learning to walk or crawl often fall, which causes single bruises. Multiple bruises, involving multiple body areas, require multiple impacts. The story given to explain the multiple injuries must then include multiple incidences.

Accidental injuries require specific motor skills on the part of the child. Here are some examples:

- A fall from a bed is impossible before the child can roll over. With some exceptions, a child can't roll over until he is at least 4 months of age. It is not unusual for children to be about 6 months of age before reaching this milestone.

- A fall down the stairs isn't plausible until the child can crawl. A child doesn't crawl until about 10 months of age or walk until about 1 year of age. She generally doesn't run well until age 2 years.

- Children aren't able to turn a hot water knob until about 2 years of age.

- A child can't ride a tricycle until about 3 years of age, which is also when he can climb the stairs alternating feet.

Based on these facts, it is obvious that a 2-month-old infant cannot roll over, let alone crawl, to a radiator to sustain a burn or to a cupboard to get into a poison. A 2-year-old who has suffered severe

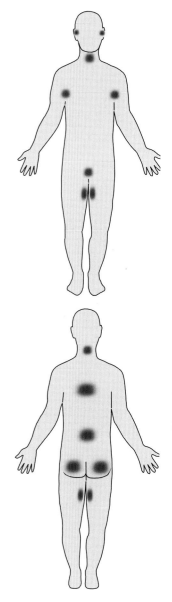

Figure 2-1. b, *Areas where abusive injuries generally occur.*

buttocks burns could not have ridden a tricycle into a space heater because he is not yet able to pedal a tricycle.

Sometimes the caretaker blames an abusive injury on another child. This can be reasonable because children are often abusive to each other. Here again you must decide if the injury could have occurred as described and if the other child is developmentally mature enough to have caused the injury. You may also want to consider whether the injury resulted from neglect or poor supervision on the part of the adult.

Many explanations of injuries can be ruled out by common sense or a sound knowledge of what happens when there are routine accidents in the home. For example, a 17-month-old child could not have burned her buttocks by climbing onto a space heater and sitting on the top. It is obvious that she would have burned her hands and legs in the climb (if she could climb).

Remember that the explanation for an injury should not change when it is questioned or challenged. If the history differs from time to time or when someone challenges it, it is very likely fabricated. For example, a daycare worker may tell her supervisor that she found a boy unconscious on the playground at the bottom of the steps. She may tell the grandmother who comes to pick him up that she found the child convulsing on the floor of the bathroom. In one case, a babysitter explained the injuries to the hands of his 5-month-old charge as rat bites. When the child's mother told him that the injuries didn't look like rat bites, he said that they were probably caused by a neighbor's puppy who often played with the child.

Some people do not consider any discipline of a child as child abuse. They consider the parents' intent and note that parents usually believe they are doing what is best for the child. Unfortunately, the injured child is not aware of the parents' good intentions.

FALLS IN THE HOME

Usually children suffer only minor injuries when they fall in the home, such as out of bed, from a sofa, off a chair, or down the stairs. If there is an object involved, such as a tricycle or stroller, it can influence the severity of the fall. Occasionally, in routine falls, the child may suffer a single skull fracture, so if your child has a significant fall, you should seek a doctor's help. But generally, major injuries do not occur in routine falls. **If the caretaker says the child had a simple fall but the child's injuries seem severe, suspect child abuse.**

Injuries caused by a fall from a vehicle, such as a bicycle, generally include cuts and scrapes. These wounds are usually dirty and contain gravel, tar, dirt, and other particles from the road or other paved surface. Injuries with this type of accident can be on multiple body surfaces because, depending on the vehicle's speed, the child may roll when she strikes the ground. The child's clothes should also show evidence of the experience. In the case of a fall from a car, such accidents are usually reported to the police. **If you are told by a caretaker that your child was injured in a fall from a car but the police are unaware of any such accident, suspect child abuse.**

SKIN INJURIES

In your role as a teacher or daycare worker, you may see a child who shows symptoms of physical and/or medical neglect. Suspect abuse:

- If a parent doesn't bring the child to a doctor when the child has a skin infection and the illness has been present long enough for the parent to have sought medical attention

- If the child's condition is not improving with the treatment prescribed because, assuming that the diagnosis and treatment are correct, the parents are probably not giving appropriate care

As a parent, it is your responsibility to seek proper medical care and follow treatment guidelines for the health of the child. Failing to do these things is abuse.

When you see an infant who is always unclean, you may be seeing a sign of neglect. But there are degrees of uncleanliness. Most infants become dirty during normal play and can be cleaned in a simple bath. The degree of dirty that suggests neglect requires several baths to begin to remove it. You may notice an offensive odor to the dirt. **If you find feces and dirt in the skin folds of an infant and under her nails, suspect neglect, which is a failure to provide for the child's basic needs.**

Diaper rash can also be a key to attentiveness and care attitudes. The skin of some infants is more sensitive than others, and some irritation and redness will occur. Diaper rash in these cases shows evidence of being cared for and seldom reaches the point where the skin is peeling, cracked, and bleeding. **An infant with a constantly dirty genital area who is left in wet diapers long enough for ammonia burns to occur is not being cared for adequately.**

Be sure to notice if your child has multiple cat or dog bites and scratches or multiple bites from other children when he returns from daycare. This may indicate that the child is being left unattended for long periods of time.

The skin can also reveal deeper injuries. Bleeding into tissues, such as muscle, will work its way to the surface. Blood that accumulates under the skin will be evident for a number of days. As the wound ages, it changes color. The color of a fresh injury is red to blue. In 1 to

3 days, it becomes deep black or purple. In 3 to 6 days, the color changes from green to brown. In 6 to 15 days, it passes from green to tan to yellow to faded and finally disappears. The younger the child, the quicker the color resolves. **If you see multiple bruises or bruises in inaccessible places, suspect child abuse.**

PATTERNS AND LOCATIONS OF INJURIES

Bruises and areas where there are clusters of pinpoint-sized red dots reveal abuse when they occur where the body is unlikely to have been injured accidentally. Multiple bruises and bruises of the buttocks or the genital area are also usually not accidental. Bruises in different stages of healing result from repeated trauma; if the caretaker gives you a history describing a single accident, it is obviously false. The evidence that trauma occurred at various times is proof that cannot be altered by interpretation. **Any significant discrepancy between the physical findings and the history is a cardinal sign of abuse. If you find that the story you are being told does not match the injury you see, suspect abuse (see Figure 2-2).**

If your child comes home with bruises that take the shape of a recognizable object, the injuries are often not accidental. Loop marks are caused by a flexible object, such as a belt, electric cord, or clothesline, folded on itself and used to beat the child **(see Figure 2-3).** Multiple curved loop marks on the child are classic signs of abuse. These bruises are usually red welts but they can be deep enough to be called cuts or scrapes. A hand imprint on a child's face after a slap, or finger and thumb marks on an arm or leg where he or she was grabbed or squeezed, are inflicted injuries. Belt buckles and other man-made objects leave recognizable imprints on the child's skin. A rope leaves characteristic signs. Rope burns, bruises, or scars around the arms, ankles, neck, or waist are evidence that the child was tied **(Figure 2-4).** Many of these injuries leave long-lasting scars. You should be aware that some caretakers have tied a boy's penis to prevent bed-wetting or pinched it as punishment for soiling **(Figure 2-5). If you see any of these injuries, suspect abuse.**

You may have been told that your child seems to bruise easily as an explanation for the injuries you find. You should report this to your pediatrician, who can order coagulation studies. Bleeding disorders, such as hemophilia, are usually diagnosed at an early age but occasionally a mild form will not be seen until the child is older. The usual age for a bleeding disorder to become evident is when the child

> "Any significant discrepancy between the physical findings and the history is a cardinal sign of abuse."

begins to walk and cruise. This, coincidentally, is also the age when child abuse is most prevalent.

What if you find bite marks on your child? The locations of bite marks on infants tend to differ from the locations on older children. Abusive bite marks around the genitalia or buttocks are usually seen in infants and are inflicted as punishment. In older children, bites that are associated with an assault or sexual abuse are often multiple and random.

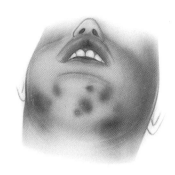

Bite marks are identified by their shape and size. Generally, they are ovoid areas with tooth imprints. The front teeth give the bite mark its shape, which matches the dental arch. No one tooth will stand out (unlike the case with animal bites, where the canines are prominent). The incisor teeth leave narrow rectangles. The marks left by the canines are triangular, and the marks made by premolars are round. It is usually possible to distinguish a child's bite from an adult's bite by its size.

If you look closely at the bite mark, you may see a suck mark and a thrust mark. The suck mark is caused by pulling the skin into the mouth, creating a negative pressure. The thrust mark is caused by the tongue as it pushes against the skin, which is trapped behind the teeth. The inner portion of the mark can show no abnormality or contain the suck or thrust mark. These two marks resemble a bruise in the center of the mark. **Bite marks are intentional injuries and are strong indicators of abuse.**

Hair loss can also be a sign of child maltreatment. Children may pull each other's hair out during play, but caretakers can also pull hair. They may use the hair as a handle to grab the child and jerk or drag him or her. Pulling can cause bleeding under the scalp, which has a rich supply of blood vessels. **If you see an accumulation of blood under the scalp in an area where your child's hair has been pulled, suspect abuse.**

Extreme cosmetic practices can also cause hair loss. Among these practices are tight braiding or ponytails; the use of tight rollers, barrettes, head bands, or rubber bands; hair straightening practices such as teasing or pulling, or frequent brushing with nylon bristles; and the use of hot combs and petrolatum. Other common causes of traumatic hair loss include pressure, as is seen on the back of infants' heads who lie on their backs or who are in the habit of "head-banging"; prolonged bed rest in one position in chronically ill persons or neglected children; thermal or electric burns; repeated vigorous massage; and severe blows to the scalp.

Figure 2-2. Child with multiple bruises involving multiple surfaces, in relatively inaccessible places, and in various stages of healing.

If you find patches of hair loss in your child, contact a doctor, who can evaluate the situation and determine if there is a medical problem or if the hair loss represents abuse.

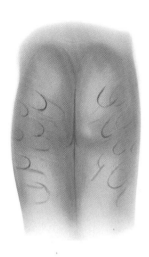

Figure 2-3. Loop marks caused by whipping with an extension cord.

Figure 2-4. Circular bruising of the wrist caused by restraints.

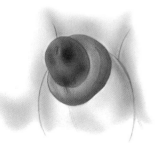

Figure 2-5. Broken blood vessels and bruising of the penis caused by pinching. The child was disciplined for soiling himself.

DROWNING

One of a parent's worst nightmares is having your child drown. If your child drowns while in the care of a babysitter or other caretaker, you should ask questions to determine if the death was indeed accidental or represented intentional harm or neglectful care. Accidental drownings usually involve toddlers or older children in public areas—swimming pools, drainage ditches, lakes, and rivers—especially in rural areas. In cities, bathtubs are the major site of accidental childhood drownings. Homicidal drownings usually occur in the home; the victims are young, either infants or toddlers. Those who deliberately drown a child are often also abusive in other ways.

Drowning that results from child abuse is difficult to distinguish from accidental immersion or drowning that occurs from sudden unexpected natural causes. In addition, deliberate drowning is underreported because of the lack of physical evidence. Features that help to differentiate accidental from nonaccidental drowning are listed in **Table 2-1**.

An often overlooked hazard resulting in accidental drowning is the large bucket. When a child drowns in a bucket, he is generally a toddler who is tall enough to tip himself into the pail, but not large enough to knock it over. The water in the bucket is heavy enough to weigh it down and deep enough to cover the child's nose and mouth.

Table 2-1. Deliberate versus Accidental Drowning

Deliberate	Accidental
Occurs in the bathtub at an unusual time of day with the drowned child alone in the bath.	Occurs during the usual bath time when more than one child is present in the tub.
Caretakers often have a history of abusive behavior or of alcohol and drug abuse. A time of crisis, often a domestic problem, is present.	Household routine is upset, resulting in a lapse of supervision. Often older child(ren) left to supervise younger one(s).
Child is usually between 15 and 30 months of age.	Child is usually between 9 and 15 months of age.
Child is held under the water until unconsciousness ensues. There is often a delay between the event and when there is a call for help or when the child is found.	Depth of water ranges from 5.0 to 35.0 cm (2 to 4 inches). Children immersed 4 minutes or less generally survive; those immersed 5 minutes or longer die.

SUFFOCATION AND SIDS

What if you are told that your child has suffered sudden infant death syndrome (SIDS)? Should you suspect abuse or suffocation? The classic child who suffers SIDS is young, was previously in good health, did not have apnea or any other breathing illness, and is the only one affected in the family. With suffocation, the child has recurrent breathing problems of unknown cause, has no viral infection or serious illness, and has had a sibling die. The first time intentional suffocation occurs in a family, it is difficult to differentiate it from SIDS. Some families do have an increased chance of multiple SIDS, probably as a result of environmental factors; there is no increased risk in first cousins or in identical compared with fraternal twins. It is interesting that there are few reports of suffocation of children by men; most cases of suffocation are by the child's natural mother.

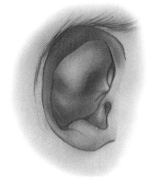

HEAD INJURIES

The child's head is a common area of injury; approximately 50% of physical abuse victims have head or facial injuries. There are very few reported mouth injuries, probably because the mouth is not usually examined. Accidental injuries to the face usually affect the forehead, nose, chin, and incisor teeth. But be aware that not all injuries to these areas are accidental.

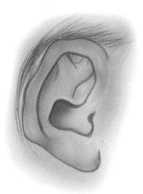

If your child suffers an injury to the ears, cheeks, temple, or bony skull area (not a single skull fracture), suspect abuse. Bleeding around the ear or ear lobe and inside the ear canal is an important sign of abuse. Cuts, bleeding, redness of the soft tissues lining the outer ear canal, or a swollen ear may be evidence of a severe blow to the ear. Such a blow may rupture the ear drum and cause hearing loss or middle ear infection.

The tin ear syndrome is caused by a slap or other blow to the ear. You may see bruises and bleeding in the cartilage areas of the outer ear **(Figure 2-6). This is abuse.**

Figure 2-6. Injuries to the ear, both old (bottom) and recent (top), caused by a blow to the side of the face. When this type of injury heals without medical intervention, it leaves a distortion of the ear's cartilage often called a "cauliflower ear."

Lip tears can occur after a direct blow to the mouth, with the tear appearing as a ragged line. Bruises, broken teeth, and facial fractures are also abusive injuries caused by a direct blow. Such injuries can also occur at feeding time. The caretaker may jam a spoon or bottle into the infant's mouth, ripping the lips. It is unusual to see injuries to other areas of the body along with this injury. Be aware that this type of tear can happen accidentally when the child, usually a toddler, strikes a sharp edge such as a coffee table. But a lip tear in an infant who is not yet walking is highly suspicious.

Lip injuries can also involve bruises, cuts, scrapes, or burns. These injuries are caused when the lip is caught between a blunt force and the teeth. Lip burns are caused by hot liquid or hot objects such as utensils or cigarettes. **All of these injuries are abusive.**

Tooth injuries are common and often accidental. If the tooth is loosened but remains in the socket and leaning, take your child to a dentist as soon as possible. If the tooth has been forced into the bone and looks shorter than the rest of the teeth, your child has suffered a severe blow to the biting surface of the tooth. The tooth may be driven completely into the bone and not be visible. When the tooth is completely removed from the socket, which happens more commonly with permanent teeth, try to locate the missing tooth; it may have been swallowed or sucked into the windpipe. The child must be taken to the dentist on the chance that the tooth can be reimplanted.

Fractures of the front teeth in children are common and usually not intentional. These fractures are caused by a sharp blow to the teeth with a hard object. This usually occurs with falling, but occasionally happens when the child is struck. Note that the missing piece may be sucked into the windpipe, so a trip to the doctor or emergency room for x-rays may be needed to locate the piece.

The tongue can be injured with a blow to the jaw when it is trapped between the teeth. Most injuries are on the sides. Teeth cut or crush and will leave jagged indentations or crushing-type injuries on the tongue. If your child says that his tongue was injured, you should check it. The best way to examine the tongue is to have the child extend it out as far as possible, then grasp the tongue with a square of gauze and pull it out as far as you can.

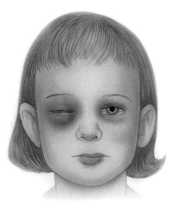

Figure 2-7. Bilateral black eyes, when there is no broken nose, must be caused by at least two blows and cannot be explained by a single incident.

Children can sustain a black eye if they fall or are struck. It is difficult to break the tissues around the eye without damaging the nose as well, unless the black eye is caused by a direct blow, such as from a fist. It is unlikely that a child will have two black eyes from a fall unless the nose is also broken. If the child falls on the center of the face, the nose will be hurt, but one or both eyes are protected **(Figure 2-7). If the history does not match the injury, suspect abuse.**

Bleeding in the upper eyelid often occurs with injury to the forehead where blood can seep down into the deeper tissues. **Bleeding around the entire eye after a forehead injury is unlikely and usually represents abuse.**

BURNS

How long does it take for a child to be burned?

- At 49° C (120° F), the lowest setting on most gas water heater thermostats, it takes 5 to 10 minutes to cause full-thickness burns to adult skin.

- At 51° C (124° F), it takes only 4 minutes.

- At 52° C (125° F), it takes 2 minutes.

- At 54° C (130° F), it takes only 30 seconds.

- Water at 60° C (140° F), probably an average temperature for most households, will take only 5 seconds to produce a scald burn. It is interesting to note that 140° F is generally the recommended intake temperature for many home dishwashers, although some commercial detergents (such as Cascade) will dissolve and sanitize at 130° F. Seattle area power companies once recommended water heater temperatures of 60° to 66° C (140° to 150° F) and their service corps set thermostats in this range.

- At 70° C (158° F), which is found in some homes, a burn through the skin will occur in less than 1 second.

Notice that we have been talking about adult skin. Children have much thinner and more sensitive skin than adults and serious burns occur more quickly and at lower temperatures. Also, if a child's skin is exposed to hot water for less time and at lower temperatures but this is done repeatedly with little time between exposures, he or she can sustain serious burns. Children may tolerate water at 49° C (120° F) for 3 minutes, but if they are left in water this hot for 9 minutes, they can suffer a severe burn.

We as parents may unintentionally expose our children to burn injuries. There were an estimated 656 cases of vaporizer-related injuries in 1979. Inhaling steam can produce severe pulmonary injury, as well as burns to the skin. Another source of accidental burning is hot floor tiles, such as those used around outdoor swimming pools. Unsuspecting toddlers are frequently victims of these hot tiles. Inside the home, children have been injured accidentally on hot registers (grating) for floor furnaces. Floor register temperatures can exceed 121° C (250° F). Wall registers may also be sources of accidental burns.

For families who live in housing complexes or other multi-unit buildings, you should be aware that the units closest to the central heating unit receive hotter water than those more distant. If the insulation is insufficient and particularly with older, less efficient heating sources, the complex's management may increase hot water temperature to satisfy the needs of families that live in more distant units, enough so that the closer units receive dangerously hot water.

Some consumer safety and/or convenience items can cause accidental burns. For example, infant automobile restraint systems are lifesaving and their use is encouraged, but you should be aware that the metal parts of the infant car seat can become extremely hot when they are left exposed to direct sunlight in hot weather.

We've been talking about accidental burns. What about abusive burns? The abuse of children by burning occurs most often in 3- to 4-year-olds or younger children and is more common among boys.

Some possible risk factors for abusive burning are listed in **Table 2-2.** These burns occur at peak times of stress in the caretaker's day.

What sorts of burns should alert you to the possibility of abuse? These are generally scalding or contact burns, where the child is either exposed to a hot liquid (usually hot water or grease) or comes into contact with a hot surface, such as an iron or a cigarette. Often you will see these burns on the buttocks, genital area, or ends of the arms and legs (called "stocking-glove" burns; **see Figure 2-8).** Usually these burns are seen in a child who also has bruises or other injuries that would lead you to suspect physical abuse. **If you see a child with burns who also has other injuries such as bruises or cuts, suspect abuse.**

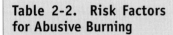

Table 2-2. Risk Factors for Abusive Burning

- The primary caretaker is educationally or culturally deprived

- The parents are unmarried or divorced

- The parents are unemployed

- The mother has been physically abused (wife battery)

- The primary caretaker is isolated, suspicious, rigid, dependent, and immature

SHAKEN INFANT SYNDROME

Shaken infant syndrome is responsible for at least 50% of the deaths of children caused by nonaccidental trauma and also causes the most severe permanent effects associated with abuse. With shaking, the child suffers a whiplash injury to the brain. The cause of injury is similar to what occurs in a car accident, which involves an acceleration-deceleration phenomenon. The skull and brain move in different directions during the shaking as the head rotates on the neck. This motion stretches and tears the blood vessels, and brain injury results.

Children who are younger than 2 years of age can suffer significant brain injury with severe shaking for the following reasons:

- The head is quite large in comparison with the body.

- The neck muscles are generally weak.

- The infant has poor control of his head and neck.

- The infant brain has a greater water content than that of an adult.

- The infant's brain is not as well protected as an adult's.

- The skull is relatively unstable, with the various skull bones not yet firmly attached to one another.

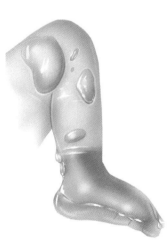

Figure 2-8. *Glove-stocking immersion burn of the foot. The sole is spared because it was in contact with the bottom of the tub. There are also splash burns on the upper leg.*

If you suspect that your child was shaken severely, look for the following signs:

Signs of Shaken Infant Syndrome

- Altered level of consciousness—the child may be sleepy, yet irritable, or may have seizures, or even be in a coma. Often the child will hold herself stiffly in an unusual posture. She can suffer respiratory arrest or die.

- Signs of shock—the child may be pale, sweating, vomiting, and listless. She may have difficulty breathing.

- Other injuries—abdominal and/or chest injuries are often present.

If these signs are present, seek immediate medical attention for your child. Try to determine how the injury occurred specifically, but be aware that if the child was shaken by an abusive caretaker, you may be given information that is misleading or false—or you may be given no information at all.

Catastrophic injuries to children are costly. One-third of these severely shaken children die; one-third, although they survive, are mentally and/or physically disabled and often require a lifetime of custodial care; and one-third have a good recovery. As we look at the three outcomes, the third—good recovery—may be the most costly. These survivors often have severe emotional problems and can become predators when they grow older, possibly becoming abusive and ending up in prison. Therefore it is important to prevent shaking and avoid the serious consequences that can occur.

Case History, with Confession, of a 2-month-old Child with Shaken Infant Syndrome

This case points out several factors about shaken infant syndrome. First, symptoms are immediate. Second, early symptoms often aren't recognized. Third, the child can appear normal after the abuse.

Shelly was a 2-month-old infant suspected to have meningitis and transferred to Cardinal Glennon Children's Hospital. Shortly after she arrived she had a seizure and stopped breathing. In the Pediatric Intensive Care Unit, the doctors found a closed head injury and bleeding in her brain and retinas. Her parents couldn't explain these injuries, but the signs clearly pointed to shaken infant syndrome.

This wasn't Shelly's first trip to the hospital. When she was 1 month old, she had a fractured leg. The parents couldn't explain that injury either, but the grandmother later said that Shelly screamed when her father was changing her diaper. State social services and the primary doctor didn't report the injury because they didn't think the family was abusive—they were so pleasant and cooperative. These health professionals believed a nurse in the hospital had handled her roughly.

On Shelly's second day in the Pediatric Intensive Care Unit, her father confessed to shaking her until she stopped crying. Here is what he said:

"On Sunday morning when I got home, I settled in. . . . At about 3 or 3:30 PM, my wife Mary went to the store to get dinner and baby formula; she was gone about 45 minutes.

"About 10 minutes later, Shelly woke up. I was watching the football game. . . . I took the bottle of formula and fed her. . . . She started choking on the formula, so I put her on my shoulder to burp her. She started crying. I couldn't get her to stop crying. I even paced the floor with her trying to quiet her. But she just kept on crying. I just got so frustrated and angry. Usually when I walk her she quiets down, but this time she didn't. I think I got too impatient with Shelly. With all the stress in my life right now, I just wanted to relax and watch the game. I couldn't handle the distraction of Shelly's crying. At one point I held her up with my hands in front of me and began shaking her back and forth. . . . I didn't even think whether it would hurt her. I just wanted Shelly to be quiet. I must have shaken Shelly back and forth about five to six times. . . . She became real limp in my hands. Her head kind of laid to one side. She stopped crying right after the shaking. Her breathing was real short like she was gasping for air. I laid her down on the couch and rubbed her belly and chest to soothe her. Shelly started breathing normally about a minute or two later. She appeared to go to sleep.

"I got up to get something to eat and just watch Shelly. . . . About 5 minutes later Shelly woke up. She was fidgeting around. I looked over at her and could see her eyes rolled "back into her head." She didn't look straight ahead. I still didn't think anything was wrong with her. A minute later Shelly closed her eyes and went back to sleep. A few minutes later Mary returned. . . .

"Around 9:30 pm I started getting ready to go to work. Shelly was still asleep. I didn't tell Mary anything about shaking Shelly to sleep. I didn't think it was a big deal. . . .

"Around midnight, Mary called and told me that Shelly had been crying for an hour and a half and she couldn't get her to stop. Mary said that she was taking the baby to the hospital. . . ."

FETAL ABUSE AND NEONATICIDE

Is there such a thing as fetal abuse? It appears that some pregnant women or their partners can directly and physically assault the fetus through the abdominal wall or via the vagina. No one knows what effect in utero physical assault has on abortion, prematurity, stillbirth, deformity, or mental retardation.

Alternatively, these individuals may express their abuse by failing to protect the fetus from an indirect assault, such as with alcohol, nicotine, or drugs. It has been estimated that the risks to the fetus from maternal alcohol and nicotine abuse outweigh the risks of other medical conditions such as diabetes. As a result of exposure to alcohol in utero, the infant may suffer fetal alcohol syndrome, with mild to moderate mental retardation, failure of certain structures (particularly those of the face) to form properly, and growth deficiencies, especially short stature and small head. Fetal alcohol syndrome is the third most common known cause of mental retardation in the United States, possibly affecting 1 in 750 live births. Studies reveal that 25% to 35% of pregnant women smoke during pregnancy, and 25% of these women smoke more than 20 cigarettes per day. Between one-half and two-thirds of pregnant women consume some alcohol, and between 2% and 13% of all pregnant women admit heavy alcohol consumption. A strong association exists between alcohol and

Table 2-3. Situations that Should be Reported as Child Abuse or Neglect

The child is reportedly injured doing something that he or she is developmentally unable to do.

The child's injury is too severe to have been caused by the incident described.

The injuries involve the backs of the hands, buttocks, genital area, abdomen, back, or sides of the body (particularly the face).

The way the injury is reported to have happened does not make sense.

The caretaker's story changes when it is challenged.

The child has suffered a severe injury but the caretaker reports only a minor fall.

There are injuries that have been left untreated.

There is evidence of neglect, such as a seriously dirty child with an odor or one with multiple animal or human bites.

The injuries are in recognizable patterns, such as a hand print or rope burn.

The child was bitten, especially in the genital area.

The child has patches of hair loss and the scalp is bleeding or has been bleeding.

The child has multiple injuries on multiple body surfaces but only a single incident is offered as explanation, for example, two black eyes and a scraped arm when the child is reported to have simply fallen down.

The child is lethargic, having seizures, or vomiting after the injury.

The child has suffered burns and has other injuries.

The child has several injuries in various stages of healing.

The child reports that he or she has been abused.

cigarette use during pregnancy. Thus unborn children are at significant risk of abuse and can be seriously harmed by their mothers' behavior.

Is fetal abuse a precursor to later child abuse? It has been hypothesized that because infants with disorders such as fetal alcohol syndrome tend to require medical care that separates them from their mothers, the normal bonding process may be disrupted, which predisposes to child abuse. While this remains to be proven, it would seem to be a reasonable assumption and an additional reason to avoid substance abuse during pregnancy.

Fetal abuse may also be triggered when a woman feels she is rejected by her spouse, family, or doctor because they direct their attention to the fetus and not her. This false perception may lead her to physically attack her "rival" or, more passively, to fail to protect or even to neglect the developing child. This is like the mechanism that produces failure to thrive in the older child. The mother neglects the child, which results in poor weight gain and stunted development. **This neglect is child abuse.**

Neonaticide is defined as murder of the infant during the first 24 hours of life. It is possible that hundreds and possibly thousands of neonaticides occur in the United States each year. Unlike women who kill their older children, mothers who commit neonaticide are rarely psychotic. Neonaticide is usually committed because the child is not wanted. It appears that the personality characteristic of "passivity" separates women who commit neonaticide from those who obtain abortions. Mothers who commit neonaticide suppress the reality of their pregnancy and make no preparations. They murder the infant when the reality of birth breaks through their defenses. Besides birth, the event that most dramatically confirms fetal existence and threatens denial is feeling the fetus move.

Why discuss fetal abuse and neonaticide in a book for parents and teachers? You may be able to save a child's life by your awareness of the dangers that can occur in a pregnancy. What steps can you take?

- If you are pregnant, avoid the use of alcohol and cigarettes, as well as other drugs.

- If you feel overwhelmed by your pregnancy, seek professional counseling to help you cope with the crisis you are experiencing.

- If you are a father, be aware of your partner's situation and provide support throughout the pregnancy and birth process.

- If you are a family member, you can help by contributing to a positive and nurturing environment for the parents and newborn.

- If you are a friend, be available to offer support and guidance as needed.

FALSE ALLEGATIONS

The alleged abuse of children, both physical and sexual, is more common in divorce and separation situations than in stable families. An allegation of abuse is difficult to deal with when it is made between separated parents and must be carefully considered. It can be a powerful weapon that one parent uses against the other or it may become a ploy to use against each other, with a call made to the abuse hotline each time the child returns. The child is caught in the middle. However, the allegation of abuse may be true and the child and family in need of help.

If you are in this situation, it is important to remember that the welfare of the child is paramount. **If the indicators of abuse discussed in this chapter are present (see Table 2-3), you should make a report to the hotline.**

CONCLUDING THOUGHTS

What should you do if your child or a child you care for has been injured or neglected?

1. *Ask questions of the caretaker. Try to get a clear idea of how the injury occurred. If possible, talk to more than one person who was present.*

2. *Evaluate whether the injury could have been caused in the way you have been told. Does the report make sense? Does it seem to fit with the child's developmental abilities? Do you feel that the situation is adequately explained?*

3. *Ask the child what happened. Listen to his or her answer and believe any report of abuse or neglect. Children, especially young children, do not generally lie about these things.*

4. *Take the child for a professional evaluation by a doctor either at his or her office or at the hospital. If you have any doubt, seek professional help.*

5. *If you seriously suspect abuse or neglect, report the incident to the child abuse hotline in your area or to the national hotline if your area does not have a local number.*

Between 1986 and 1995, child maltreatment reports have increased 49% nationwide.

Source: *Current Trends in Child Abuse Reporting and Fatalities: The Results of the 1995 Annual Fifty State Survey*, National Center on Child Abuse Prevention Research.

BEHAVIORAL INDICATORS OF ABUSE

KAREN M. BLY, R.N.

Ann received a call from the director of her son's nursery school. Her 4-year-old son, Daniel, was found in the bathroom attempting to perform oral sex on a 4-year-old male classmate. Personnel at the daycare center were appropriately concerned about the incident. The director questioned Ann about the possibility that Daniel had recently exhibited other behaviors that concerned her. Daniel was having frequent nightmares and would awaken crying. The week before the nursery school incident, Ann caught Daniel attempting to start a fire in the trash can with matches he had found. Ann also remembered that recently Daniel occasionally regressed to wetting the bed at night and sucking his thumb. He was having frequent angry outbursts and would scream, "I hate you!" to Ann.

The director of the nursery school reassured Ann that none of these behaviors was specific for sexual abuse, but they were red flags that Daniel was experiencing stress caused by something. However, the inappropriate sexual activity that Daniel displayed was a significant reason to consider that he may have been sexually victimized. The nursery school referred Daniel to a counselor who specialized in working with children.

The mindset that you should have when you are concerned about your child's behavior is to ask yourself, "What could have happened that would make my child behave this way?" Then your detective work begins and you must seek the answer by talking with your child, talking with daycare workers or babysitters, talking with other parents, and evaluating the responses you get from each one of these sources. Don't jump to any conclusion before you have all of the information possible and you have had a chance to consider the possibilities. But it is important to be aware that abuse—whether physical or sexual or emotional—is one of those possibilities.

Today, healthcare professionals and parents can obtain extensive education about child abuse. At the same time, the news media have developed a fascination with cases involving physical abuse, sexual abuse, or neglect. As a result, rarely has child abuse been alleged, suspected, reported, or diagnosed to the degree it is today.

If our world were ideal, we would not have to go further than instituting procedures to prevent abuse. Unfortunately, even with preventive measures in place, abuse exists to an alarming degree. Thus both parents and professionals must be aware of the emotional and behavioral indicators that may be seen in a child who has been or is being abused. This chapter will help parents understand behavioral indicators by looking at the following:

- ❧ *The difference between specific and nonspecific behavioral indicators*

- ❧ *General stresses that cause behavioral changes*

- ❧ *Changes that are specific to abuse—see Table 3-1*

- ❧ *Changes that are not specific to abuse—see Table 3-1*

Any sudden, unexplained change in behavior may be a warning sign that a child has been abused. Often children do not tell about abuse because they are afraid or confused; they may also be too young to explain what has happened. But when behavioral changes occur, an informed and educated parent can respond appropriately. **When the child's behavior changes significantly, one key for parents is to seek appropriate professional guidance and support to help determine what stressful event(s) created the disturbing behaviors.** Once the cause has been identified, we as parents must seek and accept appropriate professional interventions—generally counseling—for the child, the adolescent, *and* the family.

THE DIFFERENCE BETWEEN SPECIFIC AND NONSPECIFIC BEHAVIORAL INDICATORS

Before we discuss the details of behavioral indicators of abuse, it is important to remember that ***none* of the behaviors is a definite sign that abuse has occurred.** Instead, these are red flags that signal serious concern that abuse *may have* occurred. Some behaviors are more specific to abuse than others. Whether behavioral indicators exist alone or coexist with other behavioral problems, they do not prove that a child has been abused. They are only warning us that something in the child's life has created enough stress to produce unusual behavior. **Table 3-1** lists behaviors that are specific and nonspecific for abuse.

A parent who is educated and able to identify the warning signs is empowered with the ability to stop the abuse today. However, you must be careful that you do not misinterpret or overinterpret your child's behavior. While we will list and discuss the behavioral indicators of abuse, be aware that the single most significant indicator of abuse is the child's *disclosure.* In other words, **what the child says has happened is the most influential evidence that abuse has occurred.** But— you must also be careful that you do not misinterpret what your child says. You must listen carefully awhile avoiding leading questions to truly understand what he or she is communicating. (Chapter 6 gives specific help on how to talk with your child.)

> "...what the child says has happened is the most influential evidence that abuse has occurred."

Occasionally talk show hosts and hostesses present programs dealing with the subject of child abuse. These programs have effectively educated the public regarding some aspects of child abuse. With more people becoming more aware of abuse, there is a greater likelihood that the identification and prevention strategies recommended in these programs will be followed. The bad news is that the indicators of abuse and their interpretation are frequently misunderstood as *definite* signs that a child has been abused. Often when a talk show has a special presentation on abuse, our Special Assessment and Management (SAM or Sexual Abuse) team receives a noticeable increase in the number of phone calls from concerned parents. For example, a parent may call and say, "On the Monday TV special they said wetting the bed is a sign of abuse. My son just started wetting the bed 2 weeks ago. Does this mean that he's been abused?" In response to such a call, the parents are advised to have their child checked by their pediatrician for routine causes of bedwetting. Many other problems may cause bedwetting, and these must be evaluated before assuming the child has been abused. The pediatrician can check for a possible urinary tract infection or even diabetes.

Table 3-1. Behavioral Indicators of Abuse

Behaviors Specific to Abuse	Behaviors Not Specific to Abuse
Excessive masturbation	Violence
Sexual "acting out"	Sleep disturbances
Promiscuity	Fear
	Change in appetite
	Eating disorders
	Regressive behaviors
	Physical complaints
	Change in school performance
	Change in peer relationships
	Reluctance to allow exposure or examination of genital areas
	Depression and suicide attempts
	Delinquency
	Chemical abuse
	Running away
	Posttraumatic stress disorder (PTSD)

GENERAL STRESSES THAT CAUSE BEHAVIORAL CHANGES

Stresses that often create behavioral changes in children include divorce, remarriage, moving to a new school district, the birth of a sibling, the death of a relative or pet, parental loss of employment, and chemical abuse in a family unit. In addition, disasters produce worrisome behavior. Examples of disasters include the recent 100-year floods, the explosion of TWA Flight 800 or the crash of the ValuJet in Florida, the Oklahoma City bombing, and the California forest fires. Children are exposed daily to continuous, repeated news coverage of these disasters. Even though they may not personally be affected by the disaster, they experience the resulting chaos through the news presentations. Innocent television programs are abruptly interrupted for news updates, and the child's life and world are disturbed. Children watch live television broadcasts of homes slowly being crushed, burned, or swept away by raging rivers. Bombings and plane crashes create fear, panic, and desperate sadness among adults. Children are exposed to all of these feelings in their parents and are not immune to the stress they create.

If you are old enough, think back to the assassination of President John Kennedy. You can probably still recall vivid details of that day—where you were when you learned of the president's death; how everyone reacted to the news; and the resulting chaos at home and across the nation. Life as we knew it ceased to exist for several days.

Every television channel (and at that time there were only three national stations) carried coverage of the death of the president and his funeral. Schools canceled ball games, plays, and dances. Many of us had nightmares or insisted on sleeping with a night light. It was as if time stood still but the memories linger. The same holds true today—a child experiencing stresses of any magnitude may respond by developing behavioral changes.

As another example, a child whose beloved grandparent has passed away may start wetting the bed or display unusual anger toward peers or pets. These behaviors are similar to what happens when a child has been abused. Thus, the behaviors only alert us that some stress has occurred. The child may require professional counseling to determine the precipitating stress or to control the resulting behaviors.

CHANGES THAT ARE SPECIFIC TO ABUSE

Excessive Masturbation

One of the most disturbing behaviors reported by parents of children who have been sexually abused is excessive masturbation. Even 3- and 4-year-old children have been described as being obsessed with and preoccupied by masturbation. Such children masturbate frequently, with no concern for privacy. A certain amount of masturbation is normal for any child. Masturbation becomes a problem when it becomes the primary focus of the child's day and when it is done in the presence of others. When masturbation becomes excessive, abuse is one of the possible causes.

Keep in mind that masturbation initially is an innocent, self-comforting, self-pleasuring technique. A child experiencing inappropriate sexual contact may display excessive masturbation as an outcome of the abuse. A child who has never been abused but who has experienced serious life stresses may also masturbate excessively as a method to relieve stress. The young child is intellectually unable to correlate the masturbation with the relief of tension, but the masturbation can become a learned habit. As it provides comfort, relaxation, and pleasure, it is reinforced. So, although excessive masturbation is a specific indicator of sexual abuse, it is not conclusive evidence that abuse has occurred.

Sexual "Acting Out"

Sexual "acting out" may occur between a child and his peers, toys, dolls, or animals. An alarming behavior that is specific to sexual abuse is the child's sexual victimization of other children. This victimization is often associated with developmentally inappropriate sexual behavior and/or knowledge. In this situation, the child becomes the perpetrator and victimizes other children. This behavior is beyond the limits of the familiar activity of "playing doctor." "Playing doctor" immediately creates an image of children undressing and declaring, "I have a pee pee and you don't." Sexual victimization goes beyond innocent exploration and is a significant indicator that abuse has taken or is taking place. **If your child is sexually victimizing others, seek professional help for him or her.**

The child who is sexually aggressive to other children may be acting out situations that have occurred to him or her. In other words, this may be a warning sign that this is a learned behavior. Children may also reenact sexual activity they have witnessed on television or in their parent's bedroom! Remember: *do not perform sexual activities in the presence of your children. LOCK YOUR BEDROOM DOOR!* Another factor to consider is whether the child has been exposed to pornography and is acting out what was observed. **You may need to seek professional help in these cases.**

If a child coerces another child into sexual contact that is developmentally inappropriate and/or attempts vaginal, anal, or oral penetration, respond promptly. Investigate the source of such behavior. Such behavior is *not* normal exploratory behavior; it is *not* "playing doctor."

One middle-aged woman tells the story of how 10 years ago she found her daughter's dolls behind the couch with their clothes off. When questioned, her daughter said that they had their clothes off because they were making a baby. When similar situations occur today, parents often call the SAM clinic concerned that the doll scenario means that their child knows too much about sex. Logically, it follows, to these parents, that it must mean that their child has experienced sex. Be careful that you, the parent, do not overreact and misinterpret every event with sexual overtones. Clarify with your child where he or she learned this. You may be pleasantly surprised at the child's innocent explanation. Or you may be totally shocked by what may be an unanticipated disclosure of abuse.

If a child digitally (with a finger) penetrates or attempts to perform oral sex on a peer, ask the child, "Where did you learn this?" If the child replies, "Uncle Johnny did this to me," **you have reason to suspect a problem exists and should call the hotline immediately.**

Seductive or sexually provocative behavior by the child may give an adult a "funny feeling" that something has happened to the child. You should seek professional counseling.

A child may also be overly friendly to strangers and may provide indiscriminate affection. This is characterized by hugging anyone and everyone, climbing onto their lap uninvited, holding their hand, or even inappropriately touching or kissing them. One mother called recently in response to the concerns of the director of her son's daycare center. She was concerned because the child frequently tried to kiss people with his tongue. Ask the child why he does these things, and, depending on the answer, seek professional help.

Promiscuity

Often a child who has been chronically sexually abused will display promiscuous behavior. Such behavior, described as indiscriminate and unrestricted, frequently involves consensual sex with multiple partners or involvement in prostitution. **Seek professional help with these situations.**

CHANGES THAT ARE NOT SPECIFIC TO ABUSE
Violence

There are various ways you might see violent behavior in your child and all of them are worrisome. Children who have been abused, physically or sexually, often exhibit violent behavior directed at people, places, or even pets. Some of the more serious examples include torturing pets, setting fires, or injuring another child. A child who has been physically abused may interpret violence as "normal" and may react violently toward peers, siblings, or even adults. In addition, children from alcoholic families or children who have witnessed spousal abuse are more likely to react aggressively and/or violently to situations, particularly if they were also abused themselves.

Hostility and anger are common among abused children. Remember, though, that other general stresses can also create hostility and anger. A 4-year-old who is jealous of his infant brother may take his hostility or anger out on the family pet. Torturing the pet, however, is a serious warning sign that the child is having severe problems.

Sleep Disturbances

Sleep disturbances include nightmares, night terrors, fear of the dark, refusal to sleep alone, and restlessness. Children may be afraid to sleep in their own bed because they were victimized there. Or, they may fear sleeping alone because they feel vulnerable without a comforting presence. However, many children who have trouble sleeping have never been abused. **Lots of things cause sleep disturbances, and you cannot assume that the child has been abused until you have eliminated other causes.** For example, a child who awakens feeling something on his face and discovers a spider there may be afraid to go to sleep in his bed for a few days. Only by talking to your child will you uncover such information.

Fear

Fear of people, places, or activities not previously feared is another red flag. A child may suddenly react hysterically to a visit from Uncle Ed or a visit to the park. *Maybe,* Uncle Ed recently hurt the child, physically or sexually, or something happened to the child in the park. On the other hand, *maybe* Uncle Ed was strict with the child's behavior or the child fell in the park recently and that is why the child is reacting differently. **The important point is *do not* assume you know why the child is reacting in this way. Instead, carefully assess each individual situation.** *Never* directly ask the child if Uncle Ed touched him or her inappropriately. You do not want to unknowingly coach the child. However, **listen to what the child says** and give the child an opportunity to tell you what has happened. As an example, say to the child, "Tell me about your visit with Uncle Ed" or "Draw me a picture about your day at the park."

Reluctance to use a bathroom or shower may be caused by the surprise visit of a waterbug when the child recently used the bathroom. However, if there is a sudden change in bathtime behavior and/or unexplained fear, you need to carefully investigate.

Change in Appetite

A change in appetite may be either an increase or a decrease in the amount of food eaten. Often children who have been sexually abused have tremendous appetites. Some authorities believe that the child feels that gaining weight will make him or her physically less attractive to the perpetrator so that the victimization will stop. At another extreme, a child who has been forced to perform oral sex may develop swallowing problems or frequent vomiting. A physically abused child who has been force fed or even fed hot liquids may have little interest in eating anything. However, healthy, nonabused children also exhibit occasional changes in appetite and eating patterns, so you can't assume that a change in appetite is caused by abuse.

Eating Disorders

Eating disorders such as anorexia nervosa or bulimia are problems with psychological and psychiatric backgrounds. *Anorexia nervosa* is basically defined as self-imposed starvation. *Bulimia* refers to binge eating habits followed by purging, which is accomplished by self-induced vomiting and taking laxatives or diuretics.

Any child or adolescent with either of these disorders needs a thorough professional evaluation. Abuse could possibly be a trigger for these disorders. Both disorders can seriously alter the child's or adolescent's physical health and may be life-threatening without intense intervention. A famous case involved Karen Carpenter, part of a 1970s brother and sister singing duo called the Carpenters, who died of an eating disorder.

Regressive Behavior

The term *regressive behaviors* is used when a child returns to what we might call "baby behaviors," or does things that reflect an earlier stage of development. A child who has lost control of his or her world because of sexual or physical abuse may show these regressive behaviors. If your child develops such behaviors, it is a sign that he or she is under stress.

What specific behaviors are considered regressive? Children who have been toilet trained for years may suddenly start wetting the bed at night. Parents may find underwear soiled with feces hidden in closets, under the bed, or in other unexpected places. Such changes in bowel or bladder habits are significant signals that something is wrong. However, before assuming that this may be caused by abuse, *and* in the absence of a disclosure from the child, you need to take the child to his or her doctor to evaluate whether there are physical causes for this behavior. Urinary tract infections or gastrointestinal problems may cause bladder or bowel problems. Emotional stress may also be the cause. Explore all possibilities; do not focus solely on abuse as the cause. However, be alert for other behavioral indicators in association with the bowel and bladder problems.

Other behaviors that are considered regressive are thumbsucking, clinging to an adult, or talking "baby talk." Again, seek professional help if your child develops these behavior patterns.

Physical Complaints

What if your child complains of physical symptoms that are causing some degree of discomfort? Perhaps the most obvious examples of these complaints are frequent abdominal pain ("stomachaches") or headaches. Often no physical cause can be identified, but the symptoms are real and may cause frequent absences from school.

First, have the child thoroughly examined by his or her primary care physician to be sure that there is no physical cause for the symptoms. Stress may be a factor, but any possible physical problems must be evaluated before you can blame emotional factors. Also, regardless of the cause, you may need to treat the physical complaints, perhaps with medication, to give the child relief from pain or discomfort.

Changes in School Performance

Changes in school performance, grades, and behavior are frequently seen in abused children. A child who consistently arrives early to school or leaves school late *may* be avoiding an unpleasant home situation. However, he or she may also be filling a working parent's schedule needs. If you are a teacher or other concerned adult, you should talk with the child rather than assuming that the situation is related to abuse. If you are a parent who is forced to drop your child off early and/or pick him or her up late, you may want to discuss this with school personnel so that your child is appropriately supervised and cared for.

Often parents of abused children note a marked decline in their son's or daughter's school grades. Students who usually earn As and Bs start bringing home report cards with Ds and Fs. Teachers may notice that the child's homework assignments are usually turned in late or are never turned in. This may result from poor concentration, excessive daydreaming, and/or decreased attention span related to the stress of abuse. You should be encouraged to know that in many cases a steady improvement occurs in the child's grades and school performance once the child has disclosed the cause of the problem and feels relieved and safe.

What Should You Do If Your Child's School Performance Declines?

- **Talk to your child to help him or her feel the freedom to confide in you.** Chapter 6 offers some excellent suggestions for talking to your child in these situations.

- **Talk to the child's teacher(s) and/or counselor and try to determine if there is a school-related cause for the change.** Keep the lines of communication open and be responsive to the efforts of teachers and counselors to help.

- **If there is a physical or emotional problem that is distracting the child and affecting his or her school performance (for example, she cannot see the board or cannot seem to concentrate), seek medical help.** Your son or daughter may need glasses or may suffer from a learning disorder that can be addressed medically or with counseling.

- **Remember—a decline in school performance is not always caused by abuse.** Be sure to evaluate all these other areas before deciding that this must indicate abuse.

Changes in Peer Relationships

Peer relationships may become fragile at various times in a child's life. However, this is also a sign that accompanies abuse. The child's behavior may negatively affect friendships and test peers' level of tolerance and patience. School-aged children and teenagers may withdraw from social activities. The once-active child may now show little interest in cheerleading, sports, music, or even just "hanging out" with friends. These changes should be a warning that something in the child's life is out of balance. Meet with the child's teacher and/or school counselor seeking insight and advice in these situations. They may be able to help you sort through what is normal and what may be the result of abuse-related stress.

Reluctance to Allow Exposure or Examination of Genital Areas

Our SAM clinic regularly receives inquiries from parents who are concerned about their child's reluctance to allow them to bathe or to examine their child's genital areas. If your child suddenly becomes unwilling to allow someone to bathe him or her or to change a diaper, something may be wrong. However, be careful not to conclude that this means that the child has been abused. The child may simply have irritated genitals and resist bathing and cleaning because of the associated discomfort. Be aware that red or irritated genitalia are frequently seen in prepubertal girls who take bubble baths or shampoo their hair while sitting in the bathtub water. Although the bubble baths are given with the innocent intent of providing pleasure and fun, water with bubble bath and shampoo residue is notorious for causing genital irritation. We advise parents to avoid bubble baths completely and never shampoo the child's hair while the child sits in the tub water. As an alternative, have the child stand under a shower to shampoo hair after the bath is completed. And, if the child shows fear and resistance to genital exposure or cleansing, do not assume that he or she has been abused. Instead, have a pediatrician evaluate the child for other possible causes of the behavior.

We have been discussing the child who refuses exposure and bathing of genital areas. What about the child who appears overly compliant to your examination of his or her genitals and passively offers no resistance? Such behavior is of as much concern as that of extreme resistance. Although not specifically indicating that abuse has occurred, extreme compliance is a red flag that the child has learned to accept and allow the exposure and manipulation or examination of the genital areas. Again, talk to your child if you feel that he or she is reacting in an unusual manner to these situations.

Depression and Suicide Attempts

Children who are depressed may show symptoms similar to those seen in adults. You may see:

- **Lack of energy**

- **Reduced interest in personal hygiene and appearance**

- **Sad facial expression**

- **Minimal interaction or play with peers**

- **General "moping" around**

Parents have described their child as dull, lethargic, or even acting like a "slug." While everyone has an occasional "down day," if your child always seems sad and has lost interest in his or her daily routine, take the child for evaluation.

Self-destructive behaviors such as cutting one's self or pulling out one's own hair may be significant enough to warrant your concern. Occasionally we even see children who have carved initials on their body. This behavior is not normal and you should take the child to your pediatrician for evaluation.

> **"As a parent, take *any* suicidal threat or attempt seriously."**

Suicidal thoughts, plans, or attempts are severe behavioral indicators. **As a parent, take *any* suicidal threat or attempt seriously.** Children as young as 6 years old have committed suicide by hanging themselves or slashing their wrists. Any child of any age who threatens or attempts suicide should have an immediate psychiatric evaluation. Intervene at the "threat" stage before it becomes an attempt!

A depressed child who has been severely traumatized by abuse and whose self-esteem has been destroyed is at high risk for suicide. This is not meant to scare you, but I recall a 7-year-old girl who unsuccessfully attempted suicide three times before her parents obtained professional intervention. (This 7-year-old tried to hang herself and put a plastic bag over her head.) As already stated, take *any* suicide threat seriously.

If you as parents are in the process of a divorce, be aware that children frequently blame themselves and may suffer depression as a result. No abuse may be occurring, but the depression may be just as severe and real as with abuse. Thus, although depression and/or suicidal thoughts are not specific for abuse, they certainly are red flags that the child needs help. **Run, don't walk, to the nearest experienced professional.**

Delinquency, Chemical Abuse, and Running Away

Delinquency involves conflict with the law and illegal acts. These include property destruction, stealing, and violence against people. Delinquent behavior may result from many different environmental factors. Delinquency is often linked with running away, which will be discussed below.

As parents, we must be aware that alcoholic or drug-addicted adults make poor role models for children. If children use or abuse drugs, they may simply be copying what they have learned at home. However, peer influence is equally strong. Children can fall in with the "wrong crowd" of peers and give in to peer pressure to use drugs.

Children may also turn to drugs as an escape from dealing with being victims of abuse. They may view the drugs as an acceptable coping mechanism to numb themselves to the emotional effects of abuse. These children don't have to "feel" anything while they are high on drugs. It is almost like the drugs have an anesthetic effect—dulling the emotional pain that they feel.

If delinquency and chemical abuse fail to "solve" the child's problem and he cannot cope with the situation, the next logical step (from the child's point of view) is to run away from the problem. Children or adolescents incorrectly think that they can find peace by running away and avoiding the problem.

What children really need when they feel they must escape a problem using one of these methods is professional counseling and a supportive home environment (see Chapter 8). **If your child is involved in any of these behaviors, seek professional help immediately.**

Posttraumatic Stress Disorder

Most adults are familiar with the term *posttraumatic stress disorder (PTSD)* in relation to Vietnam or Persian Gulf war veterans. Unfortunately, anyone of any age can experience PTSD in response to major traumatic stress. Rape or sexual abuse can certainly be counted as major traumatic stresses, and infrequently, a child or adolescent will respond with PTSD.

What does PTSD look like in a child?

- The child often relives the trauma over and over in his or her memory.

- He or she may have sleep disturbances or difficulty concentrating.

- The child may avoid activities or places that bring back memories of the event.

- The sleep disturbances and difficulty concentrating get worse when the child's memories are triggered.

What should you do? **Seek counseling, with the awareness that this may be a long-term process.**

CONCLUDING THOUGHTS

The intent of this chapter has been to educate and inform you as parents—not to cause panic about each behavioral change you see in your child. **Remember—no behavioral indicator is clear evidence that your child was abused.** Be cautious and avoid assuming that abuse must be the answer. Instead, we encourage you to consider these behaviors as red flags that the child has probably experienced some stressful or traumatic event and he or she is attempting to cope with it. You can take the following steps:

1. *Respond calmly and cautiously.*

2. *Respond immediately.*

3. *Talk to your child and others who may be involved and have necessary information.*

4. *Seek professional counseling for your child as indicated.*

Before the age of 18, one in four girls and one in six boys will experience some form of sexual abuse.

Source: *Current Trends in Child Abuse Reporting and Fatalities: The Results of the 1995 Annual Fifty State Survey*, National Center on Child Abuse Prevention Research.

SEXUAL ABUSE

JAMES A. MONTELEONE, M.D.

It is difficult to discuss the sexual abuse of children. Many of us feel uncomfortable discussing sexual matters in any case, but to add to that discomfort the emotions that abuse brings out creates great difficulty. However, to protect your child, you must be educated about the facts and be able to handle even this difficult topic with sensitivity to the child involved.

First, what is sexual abuse? Legally, the term *sexual abuse* is defined as follows:

Sexual contact or interaction between a child and an adult or older child (greater than 5 years of age difference) for the purposes of sexual stimulation and gratification of the adult (who is a parent or caretaker and responsible for the child's care) or of the older child

Sexual abuse is a form of child abuse and if you become aware that it is going on, **you must report it to the *state child protective services.***

What if the person who is abusing the child (called the perpetrator) is *not* a caretaker? Then the sexual activity is considered *sexual assault.* While it is not necessarily abuse, **sexual assault is a sex crime and must be reported to *local law enforcement officers.***

The specific acts that are considered sexual abuse are:

- Having sexual intercourse with an adult or older child

- Being sodomized or penetrated anally

- Having oral-genital contact

- Being fondled

- Masturbating

- Being penetrated or manipulated by the perpetrator's finger(s)

- Having the adult or older child expose himself or herself

These acts can be performed on the child (who is termed the victim) or can be done together with the child.

Of the acts listed, exposure can be the hardest to define. Families may be comfortable with nudity in the home—they may share bathrooms, share bedrooms, or live in small quarters where privacy is at a premium. Exposure becomes sexual abuse when the person who is doing the exposing is sexually aroused by it and does it specifically for that purpose.

In this chapter, we will look at the following areas:

- ❧ *Defining sexual abuse*

- ❧ *What makes a child vulnerable*

- ❧ *What the perpetrator is like*

- ❧ *How to respond when your child reports being sexually abused*

- ❧ *What to look for if you suspect your child was sexually abused*

DEFINING SEXUAL ABUSE

The acts involved in sexual abuse are generally divided into three categories: sexual assault, incest, and exploitation. Sexual assault and incest are self-explanatory; exploitation includes using the child in prostitution and pornography.

Sexual Assault

A child who has been sexually assaulted generally is crying, is bleeding, and has bruises or other injuries immediately after the encounter. The perpetrator of sexual assault is usually a man, and this is often the first time he has forced himself on a child. The child is at great risk because the perpetrator is frequently emotionally unstable. **You must make certain that the child is protected and does not return to the situation where the assault took place. The perpetrator must not have any further access to the child.**

Incest

A general description of incest would be sexual intercourse between persons so closely related that they are forbidden by law to marry. Usually incestuous abuse occurs over a long period of time and it can include a *conditioning process,* when the perpetrator gradually manipulates the child to accept this as a way of life. The perpetrator is usually a man, although women can also be perpetrators and cases involving women are probably underreported. The perpetrator is not necessarily related to the child; he may be a stepfather or a boyfriend of the child's mother, but he is the father figure or provider in the home. The classic incestuous relationship is between a father and daughter, but other common relationships include an older brother and sister, an uncle and his niece or nephew, or a grandfather and his granddaughter or grandson. Several children in the home may be involved. The practice of intrafamilial abuse can be passed from one generation to another.

With incest, there is usually no immediate physical evidence because the child often does not disclose the abuse until it has gone on for a number of years. Frequently, it is only as an adult that the victim tells of the incest. With the passage of time, it is nearly impossible to prove that abuse did take place and the situation becomes the word of the victim against that of the perpetrator, with the truth never being known.

Sexual Exploitation

Sexual exploitation is unique in that it often includes a group of participants. It can occur within a family or outside of the home, involving several adults and nonrelated children; then it is referred to as a *sex ring.* When families are involved, the whole family—mother, father, and children—can be taking part. This situation reflects a pathological attitude on the part of the parents. Exploited children need intensive intervention and psychiatric help.

> "As many as 50% of the perpetrators are known by the victims; parents and other relatives are the offenders in 30% to 50% of the cases."

WHAT MAKES A CHILD VULNERABLE?

Three-fourths of the crimes committed against children are sex crimes. As many as 50% of the perpetrators are known by the victims; parents and other relatives are the offenders in 30% to 50% of the cases. Victims come from all races, creeds, and socioeconomic levels. Boys are more commonly victimized by someone outside the home, while girls are often abused by someone within the home.

What makes a child such a frequent target? Some of the characteristics of children make them ideal victims:

- They are naturally curious, even about sex. A clever child molester can exploit this trait to lower the child's inhibitions and seduce the child into sexual activity.

- Children are instructed to respect and obey adults, so they are easily misled by adults. Also, the adult is bigger, stronger, and wiser in the child's eyes. The adult can use these suppositions to control the child's behavior.

- Children crave attention, affection, and approval. Children from broken homes and those who are the victims of emotional abuse and neglect are at greatest risk of becoming sexual victims. They are willing to trade sex for the affection and attention missing from their lives.

- Adolescents, in their desire for independence, can trap themselves into becoming victims. For example, an adolescent boy who has been victimized because he rebelliously defied his parents' guidelines is very unlikely to admit his mistake.

WHAT THE PERPETRATOR IS LIKE

An adult who prefers to have sex with children is a *pedophile*. Although these individuals are sexually attracted to children, they may also have sex with adults. Some even have sex with adults specifically to gain access to children. Pedophiles have recurrent, intense sexual urges and sexually arousing fantasies involving children. About 85% of all reported perpetrators are male, and they come from all professions and trades. Those females who have been reported are often babysitters.

Pedophiles and *child molesters* are not necessarily the same. A child molester sexually molests children, whereas a pedophile has a sexual preference for children and fantasizes about having sex with them, but if he does not act these impulses out, he is not a child molester. Some pedophiles act out their fantasies in legal ways by engaging in sexual activity with adults who look, act, or dress like children. Not all child molesters are pedophiles. A person who prefers to have sex with an adult may decide to have sex with an child, but if the sexual fantasies of these individuals do not focus on children, they are not considered pedophiles.

Child molesters may be either *regressed* or *fixated*. The regressed individual has a primary sexual orientation toward adults of the opposite sex. However, under conditions of stress, this individual may regress to an earlier psychosexual age and engage in sex with children. A fixated child molester, on the other hand, has a primary sexual orientation toward children.

About 75% to 80% of sexual abusers are known to their victims. As already noted, they are generally the father figure in the home. Although most do not want to hurt the child, they may use force or aggression in their abuse. Many pedophiles use alcohol or other drugs to lower their inhibitions before abusing children.

Although the median age when pedophiles are first convicted ranges from 30 to 35, many begin to abuse children at much younger ages. The child molester is usually a respectable, otherwise law-abiding person, who, because of this respectability, may escape detection. In fact, **the average child molester is a young, well-educated, middle-class, married, white male who is employed in a stable job at a good salary. Table 4-1** profiles the various types of molesters.

Some of the approaches that molesters use are as follows:

Seduction

The molester may court children, giving them attention, affection, and gifts over a period of time and gradually lowering their sexual inhibitions. His victims willingly engage in sex in appreciation of the gifts they have received. Those who use seduction often are involved with multiple victims, such as a group of children in the same class at school, in the same scout troop, or in the same neighborhood. This individual knows how to talk to children and how to listen to them.

Table 4-1. Types of Child Molesters and What They Are Like

Regressed molester

- Has low self-esteem and poor coping skills.
- Turns to children because they are available.
- Generally coerces the child into having sex.

Morally indiscriminate molester

- Uses people and abuses everyone he comes into contact with, so that children are just other targets for his abuse.
- Lies, cheats, or steals when it is to his advantage and believes he can get away with it.
- Uses force, lures, or manipulation to obtain his victims.
- Victims are usually strangers or mere acquaintances, but they can be his own children.

Sexually indiscriminate molester

- Willing to try anything sexual and drawn by sexual experimentation.
- Has sex with children because they are new and different.
- Victims may be his own children, and he may provide them for other adults as a part of group sex.

Inadequate molester

- Classified as the social outcast, the withdrawn individual, or the "unusual" person.
- May have patterns of behavior including psychoses, personality disorders, mental retardation, or senility.
- Becomes sexually involved with children because he feels insecure or curious.
- Views children as nonthreatening and therefore ideal for use in fulfilling his sexual fantasies.
- Often acts impulsively.

Preferential child molester

- Focuses sexual fantasies on children and has sex with children because he is sexually attracted to and prefers children.
- Needs frequent and repeated sex with children, so he has the potential to molest large numbers of victims.

He frequently selects children who are already victims of emotional abuse or neglect. The fact that he is an adult who is in authority is important in the seduction process.

Introversion

The introverted molester lacks the personality skills needed to seduce children, so he usually molests strangers and very young children. He uses little verbal communication. He usually frequents areas where children congregate and watches them, hoping to find an opportunity to engage them in a sexual encounter. To have access to children, he might marry a woman with children or have his own children.

Sadism

A sadistic molester, in order to be aroused and gratified, must inflict pain on the victim. He uses lures or force to obtain his victims. He is more likely than other molesters to abduct and murder his victims.

HOW TO RESPOND WHEN YOUR CHILD REPORTS SEXUAL ABUSE

What would you do if your daughter came home from daycare and you found blood on her panties? **It is best to ask her what happened and then follow up with the daycare personnel.** Chapter 6 outlines specific ways to communicate with your child about sexual abuse. Here we just want to list a few general observations to keep in mind:

- Do not pressure the child for an answer. If you do, the odds are that your child will give an improper answer because she feels threatened. Remember, if the child was sexually abused, the perpetrator has probably threatened harm to the child or your family if she tells. If she was not sexually abused, she may have been involved in something that you would not approve of and will feel the threat of punishment. Therefore you must maintain a calm, matter-of-fact tone and ask in a nonthreatening manner. Don't ask leading or demanding questions.

- Be aware of your child's developmental level, verbal skills, and experience. Young children think in concrete terms and may have limited concepts about numbers and times. Generally, their experiences in life are also limited and their vocabulary will reflect this. For example, if the child says, "He peed in my mouth" or "he got pee on me," he may be talking about urine because he only knows one function for the penis—to urinate—and anything that comes out of it must be urine. He may in fact be describing ejaculation. A young girl may say that "he cut me down there with a knife," although you see no evidence of a cut. The child knows how it feels to be cut with a knife and that was how it felt, so she feels that she must have been cut with a knife. Whatever it was that hurt her——and it could have been a finger, a fingernail, or a penis—it felt like a knife to her.

- Be aware of the way that children view the world. When a child talks about a situation, he concentrates on a central activity and has very limited recollection of things that were happening that were not involved in the central action. For example, a 5-year-old girl said she had climbed up on an air conditioner and saw the father of a neighbor, her playmate, sexually abusing the child. She described what she saw happening. When she was asked where this happened, she said it was in the bedroom. But the air conditioner perch overlooked the kitchen, not the bedroom. Therefore it was concluded that she was lying. It is very likely that she was telling the truth about the actions that were taking place, but the peripheral information simply escaped her attention and her memory. There is also the factor that the more time that passes since the event, the more details will be lost. Even adults miss such peripheral details, especially after a passage of time.

- Remember that children can have difficulty with number concepts and with how many times something happened. A child may easily count to 10, but he may not be able to count specific objects. Days of the week, months, and seasons frequently mean nothing to a child.

- Children do purposely lie, as any parent or teacher can readily attest. Usually they do this to get out of trouble or to avoid trouble. They may lie to protect, to deny, or to minimize what happened, or they may withhold information. What about with abuse? **It is more likely that the child will lie to *deny* that abuse took place than to admit it.** And if she is asked repeatedly about it, she may get tired of telling the same story over and over and may embellish the facts to convince or please the adults who are questioning her so that they will stop.

- Be aware that giving a description of a perpetrator is more difficult for a child, especially if he is an unfamiliar person. This is related to the child's focus on the central action rather than on peripheral details.

- Children often are inconsistent in their stories. Those who are developmentally younger are less able to relate a story consistently because they focus on the central action and not on details. Remember that it is not the small details, such as an exact age, the specific number of incidents, or the time, that are essential, but rather the fact that the abuse took place. Unlike adults, children have difficulty evaluating their speech for possible errors, omissions, inconsistencies, or contradictions. Adults tend to fill in missing pieces based on logical assumptions; children are generally too inexperienced to do this and leave the memory gaps, which make the child's testimony seem less coherent even when it is more accurate.

Are Children's Memories Reliable?

Although children recall less than adults do, what they do recall can be quite accurate. If the child understands and is more familiar with a particular event than an adult is, the child's memory is frequently more accurate.

Can Children's Stories Be Altered By Suggestions?

Children usually say so little in response to questioning that adults are often tempted to ask suggestive questions. This can lead to inaccurate answers. Children can also be persuaded to make a false statement if the person who is questioning them is of high status, such as a policeman in uniform. However, **it is more difficult to lead a child to make a false statement about the central information that he or she wants to convey than about peripheral information that he or she may not vividly recall.**

WHAT TO LOOK FOR IF YOU SUSPECT YOUR CHILD WAS ABUSED

Obviously, you should notice physical signs that indicate abuse (see Chapter 2) and specifically ask the child about them. If you are not satisfied with her answer or if she tells you there was abuse, you must follow up through the proper channels. Also, if you note any of the behavioral signs listed in Chapter 3, you should follow up.

A Special Note about Adolescents

If your child is an adolescent, sexual abuse can result in specific behaviors. Among the findings for adolescent girls who were abused as children are:

- They often begin engaging in voluntary intercourse at a young age.

- They are more likely to use drugs and alcohol.

- They tend to have sexual partners who are older and are also using drugs and alcohol.

- They are less likely to use contraception and are more likely to have had an abortion.

- They are more likely to be in a violent relationship.

- They also report experiencing emotional abuse and physical abuse in childhood.

- Finally, abused young women who have had children are more likely to report that their children are being abused.

As you can see, childhood sexual abuse has devastating effects on adolescents. Often these adolescents see themselves as living in a world full of unpredictable, random events and actions that have no rational consequences. They believe that they have no power over what happens and allow themselves to become passive actors who do not see any way to help themselves, to make better choices, or to take actions that will make a difference. **These individuals need counseling by a trained psychologist or psychiatrist.**

What About Adolescents or Young Adults Who Say They Were Sexually Abused as Children? Is There a "False Memory Syndrome"?

When children are sexually abused and do not tell about it until they reach young adulthood, some have questioned the story and labeled it "false memory syndrome." **In general, childhood sexual abuse is confirmed by a group of symptoms, such as memories, personality and behavior disturbances (see Chapter 3), and current life distress.** Therefore, when a young adult discloses that he or she was abused as a child and these other signs are present, the chances are that the story is true.

More than 50% of all victims of child abuse suffer neglect.

Source: *Current Trends in Child Abuse Reporting and Fatalities: The Results of the 1995 Annual Fifty State Survey,* National Center on Child Abuse Prevention Research.

NEGLECT AND ABANDONMENT

Wayne I. Munkel, L.C.S.W.

Some of the saddest and most disheartening stories covered in the evening news or pictured in the newspapers concern the neglect and abandonment of children. We see pictures of garbage heaped up and covering furniture, human and animal waste overflowing from nonfunctioning toilets, rat droppings on stale or moldy food, children wearing only t-shirts in sub-zero weather—conditions that no one should be forced to live in. Yet we need to recognize that unless a tragedy occurs, such as the death of a child who is left unsupervised, these situations go undetected and unreported. The following case demonstrates what usually happens in situations where neglect and abandonment occur:

A 2-year-old boy darted into the street to catch up with his 4-year-old sister and 6-year-old brother. They were late for the preschool they attended. The child did not see the approaching ambulance and his feet were broken when the tires of the vehicle ran over them. In the emergency room, a hospital social worker recognized the child's mother from previous clinic visits. Her children were being treated for lead poisoning and her infant had been treated three times in recent weeks in the same emergency room for rat bites. A call was made to protective services to report the lack of parental supervision.

In the subsequent investigation, a visit to the family home revealed it was without heat, electricity, or running water. Electricity was being stolen from a neighbor's apartment through a series of small-gauge extension cords. While investigators were in the apartment, a nest of rats was found under the kitchen sink, and several were seen in the kitchen. Their footprints could be seen in the leftover food on the table. A hot plate was the only source of heat in the dwelling. The apartment smelled of sewage and investigators found a bathroom where both the tub and the toilet were being used but were not functioning. The overflow of the tub and toilet had created a black tarry substance that covered the floor. The shoes of one investigator became mired in the black substance and he had to walk out of his shoes.

The children in the home appeared malnourished and had obviously not bathed in a long time. All of them had head lice and their hair had not been combed nor brushed in weeks. Their clothing was dirty and torn, and it was obvious that they were cold. The children were taken into protective custody. As the investigators were leaving, they heard an infant cry. Using flashlights, they found an infant in a pile of rags in a darkened room. The infant had rat bites that required medical attention.

The mother of these children was receiving nearly $1000 a month in public assistance and other income—an amount that was more than adequate to provide for her children. She was charged with neglect, convicted, and placed on probation. Her children remained in foster care for several years.

In this chapter we will present information that all parents should have about:

ॐ **The face of neglect––what it looks like**

ॐ **The factors in neglect––what produces or contributes to this behavior**

ॐ **The future of neglected children––what happens to children who are neglected or abandoned**

ॐ **The family's defenses––a check list of what we as parents can do to undergird our families**

The photographs offered in this chapter are disturbing; they show the physical effects of neglectful behaviors. But what is even more disturbing to us as parents is the fact that **most cases of neglect and abandonment are caused by parents.** So as we look at the facts concerning neglect and abandonment, we must keep in mind that the perpetrators are parents—just like us; they face difficulties—just like us; and they choose to respond in ways that are inappropriate— hopefully, not like us. We don't want to perpetuate these behaviors, but ignoring them will do just that. This chapter's purpose is to expose what has been for so long a dark secret and make us aware of the factors that can produce such behavior. Then we will look at areas where we can strengthen our families and make them as safe and supportive as possible.

THE FACE OF NEGLECT––WHAT IT LOOKS LIKE

Legally, neglect can be defined as "**reckless** failure to provide, by those responsible for the care, custody, and control of the child, the proper or necessary support, education as required by law, nutrition or medical, surgical, or any other care necessary for his well-being; and food, clothing or shelter sufficient for life or essential medical and surgical care." Each community's Juvenile and Family Courts interpret the standards of this law. In the example above, the court stated that the conditions in that home were clearly neglect. But some cases aren't as clear, as seen here:

> *A 2-month-old infant is found dead in his crib by his mother. The cause of death was suffocation. The infant shared the crib with a 2-year-old and a 4-year-old sibling. The medical examiner decided that the cause of death was accidental. One of the siblings, while sleeping, probably laid on the child, causing suffocation.*

Was neglect involved? If so, who was neglectful? The mother? No one told her the child would be in danger if he slept with others. If the mother had had more money, she could have afforded beds for each child. If she had been better educated, she would, hopefully, have known better than to put these children in bed together.

> *A mother leaves seven children in the home while she goes on a date. The eldest is 8 years old. He has been in trouble previously for playing with matches. While she is gone, there is a fire and all the children are killed. The neighbors and firemen had trouble reaching the children because the windows were barred and the door had a deadman board against it. The court decides it is an accident caused by a child playing with matches.*

Most of us would see this case as involving neglect, with the responsibility shared by the mother, the landlord, the neighbors who were aware that the mother would often leave the children alone, and the fire inspector.

Practically, neglect is the failure of caretakers to provide for the basic needs of their children. They may fail to meet these needs to different degrees, ranging from mild to severe, and the neglect itself can be a short-term or a long-term problem.

In neglect we can see the caretaker failing to meet the child's need for:

- A safe physical environment
- Adequate nutritional or health care
- Support for his or her growth and development

The examples listed below provide guidelines for caretakers. Note that in each example given, the courts have decided that these conditions are neglect.

Physical Environment

Inadequate shelter. Children need a home that provides shelter so that their other basic needs can be met. The standards for what is adequate vary from community to community but the minimums include:

- Shelter from the elements
- Heating in cold weather
- Adequate space for sleeping, eating, bathing, and playing

In a house that is too crowded with people, furnishings, trash, or garbage, children simply get lost. They may not be supervised because each adult assumes that someone else is managing the child's care **(Figure 5-1).**

> *In one home, 25 persons were living in a four-bedroom house. An 18-month-old child was injured when she fell down the stairs. The mother thought her sister was watching her child.*

Another sign of an inadequate shelter is a home that is structurally unsound.

> *A condemned building with the back wall missing was home to two women and three children. This was obviously unsafe housing, and the children were placed in foster care by the police until their mothers could find new housing.*

Inadequate sleeping arrangements. A child who doesn't get enough sleep may appear to always be tired or listless. Why isn't the child sleeping? There may be too many people living in the house, too much noise, too many people sleeping in one bed, or no beds available. When there are too many people in one bed, "layover" deaths can result, as noted in the example above. Bedding can be inadequate for cold weather or it may be soiled. A child may lack privacy from children or adults of the opposite sex and therefore be too uncomfortable to sleep. In addition, having children sleep with adults can contribute to sexual abuse.

Unsanitary conditions. The house where garbage and trash are allowed to accumulate is both unsafe for children and unsanitary. Toilets may be unusable, and there may be animal and/or human wastes on the floors of the house. Often, rats, mice, and roaches are present.

Fig. 5-1a

Fig. 5-1b

Fig. 5-1c

Fig. 5-1e

Fig. 5-1d

Figure 5-1. *The police were called to investigate the possible abandonment of nine children. They found a small apartment housing the children, ranging in age from 5 to 10 years. They were the children of two mothers who were living in a different, well-kept apartment with their boyfriends. The mothers were collecting welfare subsistence and occasionally dropped off food for the children. (**a** and **b**) The apartment housing the children was cold and had only one source of electricity, an extension cord that stretched down the hall and out of the bedroom to another apartment. (**c**) There was little food in the house; the refrigerator was not working and was essentially empty. The children were living on a combination of grease, potatoes, and pork and beans. (**d**) A frying pan, with no handle, had old lard still in it with evidence of rat prints in the grease, and the cupboard under the stove was full of rat feces. (**e**) Trash was strewn in one of the rooms. Several of the mattresses were torn.*

> *A 7-year-old child was covered in "layer dirt." The bottoms of his feet were caked with a layer of dirt and fecal material that had to be scraped off. When that was done, several infected sores were seen on the soles of his feet. Police were sent to the child's home and found the floors covered with trash and sewage.*

Structural hazards. Structural hazards can include the following:

- A house or building that has partially collapsed

- Stairs that have broken steps

- Missing railings or protective barriers on stairs, porches, or balconies

- Windows and doors in poor repair, including those with broken or jagged glass

- Missing door or window screens

- Holes in floors and ceilings

- Floors badly worn and covered with large splinters

> *An 11-year-old girl leaned against a second-story porch railing. The rotting rails gave way and the child suffered fractures of her skull and face. The girl's mother had tried to fix the problem by telling her landlord, but nothing had been done.*

What could the mother have done in this situation? Since contacting the landlord had not produced results, she might have blocked the child's access to the porch both physically and verbally by warning the child to stay off of it, or she might have tried to repair the railing herself or with the help of friends or neighbors. These acts would have required very little effort compared to the injuries the child suffered.

Inadequate housekeeping. Dirt and filth are present, especially in the kitchen and bath. Clutter and trash have been allowed to accumulate over a long period of time. While anyone can have temporary clutter, in neglect situations, the caretakers make no attempt to clean up or remove the mess.

Fire hazards. Exposed or frayed wiring, fuel containers stored in living areas, and combustible materials placed near heat sources are common hazards. When beds are placed too close to heat sources, children can suffer burns or fires can be started. Metal bars on windows and "deadman" props against doors trap people inside when there is a fire in the house.

> *Three children were left alone while the mother went to the store. A fire started in an upstairs bedroom. When firemen arrived, the door to the upstairs was blocked with a board between the door handle and the stairs (**Figure 5-2**), so the firemen had to break through the door. All three children recovered, but firemen estimated that they were seconds away from death.*

Substance accessibility and use. Leaving chemicals or drugs within the reach of children or where they can easily get to them can be neglect. Having illicit drugs in the house and using the house in drug traffic are particularly hazardous when children are around. Each year thousands of children are poisoned when they ingest household chemicals and drugs in their homes or in the homes of other people.

> *A 2-year-old child who woke before his parents was found intoxicated, having drunk some of the alcoholic drinks left over from a party his parents had hosted the night before.*

Fig. 5-2

Figure 5-2. *Safety hazard—deadman bolt at the back door, making exit from that point impossible.*

This situation could occur in any home where adults have parties and alcohol is consumed, so the danger is not limited to homes where neglect is a way of life. We as parents need to be aware of the hazard to young children in these cases and make the effort to clean up at least to the point where children do not have access to intoxicating substances. Although we may see intoxicated adults as amusing, children who become intoxicated represent a serious situation.

Excessive hot water temperature. Each year children are burned by excessively hot water. The scenario is remarkably similar: The bath water is started. The caretaker leaves the bathroom to answer the phone or the door, or to attend to another child. The child is heard crying in the bathroom. Rushing back to the bathroom, the caretaker finds a child with severe second-degree burns. **You should be aware of the time required to produce a second-degree burn and make sure that the hot water in your home does not exceed 120° F.** Chapter 2 outlines specific information about burns.

Nutrition and Health Care

Nutrition. Children require food that meets their nutritional needs and is appropriate for their age and stage of development. Children may suffer when they have poor quality food, food that lacks in nutritional value, or food that is not from various food groups, meaning that there is not enough variety (too many carbohydrates or sweets and not enough vegetables, meats, fresh fruits, or dairy products). An adult caretaker may not prepare meals consistently or may provide foods that are inappropriate for the child's age and level of development. Besides providing the right types of food, caretakers should make meal time a pleasant experience, but in some homes it is chaotic and stressful for the child.

Clothing. Children need clothing that is adequate and appropriate for the weather and the season. If the clothing is dirty, does not fit well, or is torn or worn out, the child may suffer in the rain or cold. The child's shoes must be adequate for the season, of the right size, and in good shape.

A 6-year-old child walking to school in below-freezing weather had only a long-sleeved shirt and long pants and tennis shoes. His feet were wet from the snow, and he was obviously cold. His teacher called protective services to report possible neglect.

Supervision. Lack of supervision is the single largest category of neglect. Children may be injured repeatedly simply because the caretaker is not paying attention. Children can also get into substances, even legal medications, that are toxic and suffer poisoning. When can children be left unsupervised? Although it differs by state, several state laws specify age 12 years. Basically, you can use the guideline that **children who cannot care for themselves must be supervised.** As a child gets older, he can be left alone for longer periods of time. Generally, parents are the best judges of the maturity and responsibility levels of their children.

Personal hygiene. As children grow, they need to be taught personal hygiene and be provided with the tools for self-care. Children who have not bathed for a long time, which is usually evident by the smell of urine, feces, sweat, crusted dirt, or unkempt hair, may be neglected children. Poor hygiene can also result in severe dental caries and mouth odor.

Medical neglect. Children's health care needs vary from individual to individual, according to genetics, and by chance. But all children need regular checkups and immunizations. In addition, children who have diseases or conditions that are not cured often have special needs for medical care. When the child is neglected, minimal health care is not obtained and the child lacks immunizations. Often there is too little or too much reliance on emergency services. The caretaker may not obtain prescribed medicines or equipment, and ignores dental needs. The treatment for chronic physical or mental illness is not followed or is not followed in a way that helps the child get better. You should know that when law and religion intersect over immunizations, blood products, pain medications, or other specific treatments, legal provisions generally favor having the court intervene on behalf of the child.

Support for the Child's Growth and Development

Education. According to state law, children must be enrolled in school between certain ages, usually in the range of 7 to 16 years. But some caretakers permit chronic truancy and do not encourage going to school. In addition, the caretaker may fail to provide the necessary control, discipline, or role model for learning, socialization, or responsible behavior. In the situation of home-schooling, parents are required to work within the laws of their state.

Emotional neglect. To really be healthy, the child must have the caretaker's emotional support and encouragement. Caretakers who are unable to show emotions, who are indifferent, or who reject the child are guilty of neglect.

FACTORS IN NEGLECT—WHAT PRODUCES OR CONTRIBUTES TO THIS BEHAVIOR

Neglect and abandonment can occur because the caretaker does not form an attachment to the child, which is termed *bonding.* Normally this develops while the mother is pregnant or when the child is born. Because the bonding does not occur, the caretaker does not have a sense of being responsible for providing for the child's basic needs.

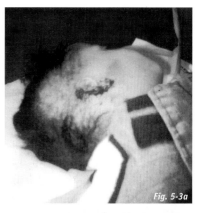

Fig. 5-3a

Abandonment is a legal term and has legal implications. Generally, abandonment is leaving the child in such a way that no provision is made to meet the child's needs or, if he or she is left in the care of another person, the parent or caretaker does not return and take responsibility for the child. Adults who abandon children tend to engage in sexual promiscuity with or without alcoholism, have financial problems, and be in a poor state of health. Depression, especially when severe, can also be a factor in causing abandonment. Another aspect of abandonment involves leaving the child with unsuitable caretakers, as occurred in the case depicted in **Figure 5-3**. It is important to know your caretaker well and leave children in the care of responsible, mentally and emotionally healthy individuals.

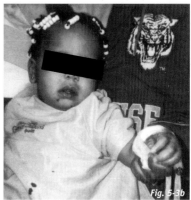

Fig. 5-3b

Figure 5-3. These two children, both less than 1 year of age and living in a multi-family dwelling, were left in the care of a psychotic adult who bit the earlobe of the 11-month-old boy *(a)* and the end of the 9-month-old girl's little finger *(b)*.

At its worst, abandonment can result in *infanticide.* In these instances the infant is left to die or is left in conditions likely to result in death. The six types of abandonment are listed in **Box 5-1.**

Box 5-1. Six Types of Abandonment

- Fatal or near-fatal abandonment: the child is left to die

- Abandonment with physical needs provided by others: the child is left with others and the caretaker does not return

- Throwaways: the child is locked out of the house or otherwise put out on the street

- Refusal of parental custody: the child is shuffled from one caretaker to another, with no one taking responsibility for his or her care

- Lack of supervision: the child is left in an unsupervised situation

- Emotional abandonment: the child does not receive any emotional support or love from the caretaker

Examples of these behaviors include the following:

Twin infants were put in trash bags and placed in a dumpster by the mother, who called the father and told him where they were. He rushed there in time to save them. Unfortunately, a few months later one of the twins died of suspected SIDS.

A child was placed in a gangway in subzero weather by a young mother. The toddler's crying alerted a passerby who found the child.

A 2-year-old was found, bound hand and foot, in a suitcase under a hospital dumpster by a security guard. The child had slipped the gag off her mouth and cried for help. The child had been kidnapped in another city by rival prostitutes and left to die.

A newborn infant was found by a security guard when he looked into a gym bag he found on an icy street in a public park.

A mother who already had six children removed by child protective services personnel gave birth to an infant in December. She walked five blocks and left her newborn in a dumpster. Four hours later, a man taking out his trash heard the infant's weak cries. The infant recovered and was placed in an adoptive home.

Failure to thrive is the condition produced in a child when the parent or caretaker fails to provide the nurturing atmosphere the child needs to grow and do well. **Box 5-2** outlines the typical appearance of a child who is not thriving.

Box 5-2. Signs and Symptoms of Failure to Thrive

- A failure-to-thrive child is thin and emaciated.

- He may have a pot belly, have limp, weak muscles, suffer episodes of diarrhea, seem to be tense and miserable, and have cold, dull, pale, and splotchy skin.

- These children are apathetic and withdrawn, they tend to avoid personal contact, and they do not respond emotionally and verbally, often even avoiding eye contact.

- They may have short temper tantrums.

- Many appear to be insensitive to pain and have self-inflicted injuries.

- Some still wet their beds and soil their underclothes long past the age when most children are toilet trained.

- Insomnia and disrupted sleep are common, so these children often roam around at night, probably searching for food. Some eat and drink inappropriate substances from the garbage can, toilet bowl, or the dog's or cat's dish.

- These children often have feeding and behavioral problems.

- Infants in these families become withdrawn, undemanding, and unresponsive.

Researchers have looked at family dynamics to try to understand what causes children to fail to thrive. What they have found is that it is possible for infants and children to starve to death in front of their parents and not be recognized. How can this happen? The major factors that seem to play a role are:

- Parental attitudes

- Deficient social support networks

- Poor or absent parenting skills

These factors work together to create an environment where parents are simply blind to their child's distress. When they are asked about the child's condition, they deny that there is a problem. If the family does not get treatment, the child who fails to thrive, and is therefore smaller and less able to defend himself, can be targeted for physical abuse, which can be severe enough to result in the child's death (**Figure 5-4**).

Figure 5-4. This 11-year-old boy with cerebral palsy was taken from a foster home. The foster parent ran a child daycare center. A second child, also with cerebral palsy, had been in the same foster care and was found dead with evidence of severe malnutrition. The foster parents denied neglect, saying that the child was difficult to feed because of the cerebral palsy. The foster parents said that the boy's rapid weight gain in the hospital was due to the specialized care by the experienced nursing staff there. Employees in the daycare center said that the two children were kept in a secluded room alone all day. Feeding was done only by the foster parents. The foster father confessed that the children were often poorly fed. He also admitted that when the boy was in the home, he was often locked in a closet. The boy is severely malnourished *(a)*. You can see the difference between the old weight measurements and the weights recorded during recovery *(b)*. A picture of the child before he went into foster care *(c)* also shows the extent of the neglect. (Photographs published with special permission from the child's parents.)

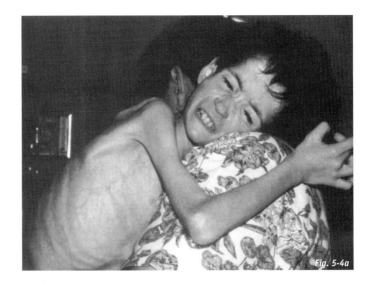

Fig. 5-4a

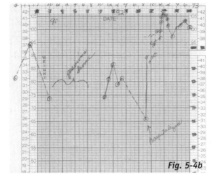

Fig. 5-4b

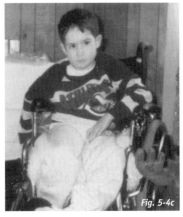

Fig. 5-4c

Exposure to toxins. Prenatally, mothers are told to avoid toxins that could be harmful to the developing fetus. Among these toxins are nicotine and alcohol. Poor nutrition and cigarette smoking are known to cause lower birth weights in infants, and the effects of alcohol include *fetal alcohol syndrome,* where the child can suffer long-term problems. Other hazards include:

- Heavy metal intoxication, which can occur on the job and causes brain damage and impairment of other systems in the developing fetus. Adults can be exposed to lead working with lead-based paint in the automobile industry, in the manufacture of storage batteries, or in printing; exposed to arsenic in farming situations where arsenic-containing sprays, pesticides, or weed killers are used; or exposed to thallium in the manufacture of optic glass, prisms, industrial diamonds, or fuel additives for internal combustion engines. They may be accidentally exposed to heavy metals by drinking whiskey distilled in lead-containing pipes, in burning batteries as cheap fuel, while hand mixing lead-based paints, or by drinking substances containing rodent killer. Pregnant women should be aware of occupational hazards and

Fig. 5-5a

Fig. 5-5b

Fig. 5-5c

Figure 5-5. *This case involved a drug raid. Five children, ages 2, 5, 7, 9, and 10 years, were found in the home along with six adults, who were arrested on drug charges. **(a)** The police found potent drugs as well as marijuana. **(b)** There was trash all over the house. The tub was clogged and filled with waste, as was the toilet and a five-gallon plastic container under the bathroom sink.*
***(c)** Drug paraphernalia was in reach of the children, and an open, full gasoline can was in one of the rooms. The crib was next to the space heater.*

request reassignment if they are in danger of exposure. They should avoid accidental exposure by not engaging in risky behaviors. Children can also be exposed in some situations, particularly in accidental cases, and we need to make efforts to store such chemicals safely.

- Rubella, which is known to cause birth defects.

- Use of illicit drugs, such as heroin, marijuana, amphetamines, cocaine, and crack cocaine, that harm the fetus.

You should also know that caretakers who are under the influence of drugs or alcohol commit thousands of neglectful and abusive acts each year. In addition, drugs and alcohol facilitate the sexual abuse of children by lowering inhibitions in both the adult and the child. The purchase of these substances also affects the lives of children because it diverts financial resources from providing for the family's basic needs. Finally, the use of drugs in the home or having caretakers who traffic in drugs can have demoralizing effects on children. The values of the home contradict those of society and can leave the child confused and in conflict, not to mention the possibility that the child may be victimized by the people who are coming and going from the house **(Figure 5-5).**

What can you do if you see these situations occurring? **If you are a family member or friend who sees children being abused by caretakers who are under the influence of drugs or alcohol, report the case to authorities and seek help from the agencies listed in Chapter 13 of this book. If possible, remove the child from the dangerous situation as quickly as you can.**

Families are but one context in which neglect occurs. These families live in a society that neglects. The social welfare programs that in the past offered support for families have been reduced or dismantled in the last decade. Many of these services reduced stress factors known to be associated with neglect, such as insufficient income, inadequate housing, social isolation, family discord, and the use of drugs and alcohol. The loss of these supportive services has stressed families even more. In addition, cuts in funding for education, mental health, and public housing as well as limited access to medical care have increased the incidence of child neglect. As stated earlier, the drug problem and associated crime have led to the deaths of children and extreme physical neglect.

THE FUTURE OF NEGLECTED CHILDREN—WHAT HAPPENS TO CHILDREN WHO ARE NEGLECTED OR ABANDONED

Child neglect hurts. Neglected children suffer hurts in their bodies, their minds, their emotions, and their spirits. The hurts in their bodies can mend and heal but the hurts in the mind have far-reaching ramifications. We recognize the hurt mind as delayed intellectual development in preschool and school. Hurts in their emotions are exhibited by aggression and depression. When the spirit is hurt, the child no longer tries and instead withdraws from life. The joy of childhood is lost.

Failure to thrive produces specific effects. Among these are physical and developmental retardation. The early years of life are critical periods of development for the child. Neglect can cause development to stop or be delayed. Children cannot be put in an emotional deep freeze or placed on hold while the caretakers work on the causes of neglect.

Extreme neglect can result in the child's death. Children who do not die from neglect may suffer from long-term problems. The effects of malnutrition, for example, include lower intelligence, slowed growth, poor teeth, deformities, and lifelong poor health.

Children who have been neglected have increased psychological problems. They tend to have disorders involving social misconduct, difficulty relating to others, and slowness in thinking processes. In abandoned children who suffer failure to thrive, the parent's lack of nurturing and attachment produces a similar response in the child, perpetuating this cycle.

Adults who were neglected as children have trouble extending trust, adult relationship problems, low self-esteem, and impaired social skills. It has been noted that mothers who neglect their children seem unable or are unwilling to provide for the health, safety, or well-being of their children. In turn, their children have difficulties pulling themselves together to deal with various tasks.

Whether extreme or subtle, neglect creates unhappy, unproductive, and sometimes violent adults.

> **"When the spirit is hurt, the child no longer tries and instead withdraws from life. The joy of childhood is lost."**

The Family's Defenses--A Check List of What We As Parents Can Do to Undergird Our Families

It is possible to break the intergenerational cycle of neglect. Currently, most efforts in preventing neglect have been *secondary prevention,* which means that once a neglected child is recognized, efforts are made to prevent further neglect and to treat the harm already done to the child. *Primary prevention* of neglect is possible if the families who are at risk are found and connected to resources that provide programs to support them and work to eliminate the factors that product neglect. The aim of primary prevention is to intercept neglect before it occurs. Areas where programs are targeted include environmental and safety interventions, the early identification of problems in bonding, parenting problems, family stresses, emotional support issues, and parenting skills.

The goals for these programs include safer homes, educated parents, stress reduction, parental skills training, and, for some, the permanent removal of children from unsafe conditions. Unfortunately, primary prevention of neglect is generations away even if we start now. But we must recognize that treatment of the victims of neglect can be the primary prevention of a future generation. Treatment of the neglecting parent or caretaker can also decrease the damage in the present. Chapter 13 offers resources for parents, grandparents, other relatives, and friends who are concerned about neglect and abandonment issues.

> **Check List for Strong Families (see also Chapters 6 and 8)**
>
> ❑ Be actively involved in prenatal preparation, including screening and checkups, before your child is born.
>
> ❑ Spend time with your children, giving them the supervision and guidance they need at each developmental stage.
>
> ❑ Be aware of your child's needs for physical, emotional, social, and spiritual growth and offer patience and support.
>
> ❑ Stay focused on what is important and seek healthy ways to relieve stress and provide enjoyment of life.
>
> ❑ Ask for help in areas where you feel inadequately prepared.
>
> ❑ Model the types of behavior that you want in your child.

FUTURE HOPE

The establishment of family support centers shows promise in meeting the challenge of parenting in today's society. These centers are located in neighborhoods where families who need them can turn for help. Their focus is on families and on providing the services that families need. Coordinated efforts in managing and treating child abuse and neglect are located in some of these centers.

All states have established funding sources for child abuse and neglect prevention services. It may be that we have finally realized that it is less costly to prevent abuse and neglect than to pay again and again—indeed, many times over—for its results.

SUGGESTED READINGS

Mayhall, PD, and Norgard, KD: *Child Abuse and Neglect: Sharing Responsibility,* John Wiley & Sons, New York, 1983.

Study Findings (NIS-1): *National Study of the Incidence and Severity of Child Abuse and Neglect: 1981,* U.S. Department of Health and Human Services, Washington, D.C., 1981.

Study Findings (NIS-2): *Study of the National Incidence and Prevalence of Child Abuse and Neglect,* U.S. Department of Health and Human Services, Washington, D.C., 1988.

In 1996, 53% of all victims of child abuse in the U.S. were white; 27% were black; 11% were Hispanic.

Source: U.S. Department of Health and Human Services. *Child Maltreatment 1996: Reports from the States to the National Child Abuse and Neglect Data System,* Washington, D.C.: U.S. Government Printing Office, 1998.

TALKING TO CHILDREN

Vicki McNeese, M.S. and Theodore A. Henderson, M.D., Ph. D.

Case 1. *A 3-year-old girl, Jill, tells her 9-year-old cousin that Uncle Scott "sexes her." The cousin tells her mother who subsequently informs the young girl's parents about Jill's initial statement. The parents are extremely upset and angry. Jill's father physically attacks Uncle Scott. When Jill is questioned about her statement to the cousin, she repeatedly denies anything happened to her. The parents request that Jill be interviewed by a therapist with expertise in evaluating young children for possible sexual abuse.*

During the evaluation, Jill states that she is afraid her mommy won't love her anymore. Further inquiry reveals that the alleged perpetrator told Jill that if she told her parents about his abuse of her, her father would be very mad at her and her mother wouldn't love her anymore. It was not surprising that when Jill saw her father get very mad, she would fully expect that her mother would not love her anymore. After her mother reassures her that she would love Jill no matter what might have happened, Jill discloses multiple incidents of sexual abuse by her uncle. Jill's 5-year-old brother, Ben, subsequently discloses that he has also been sexually abused by the uncle. Ben says that he was afraid he would be in trouble for not telling his parents when they first asked about abuse.

Case 2. *A 4-year-old girl, Sara, whose parents are divorced, returns from a weekend visit at her father's home with a reddened, irritated vaginal area. Sara rubs her vulva excessively, complains that her "pee pee" hurts, and refuses to allow her mother to wash her genital area during bath time. Sara's mother is worried that Sara may have been sexually abused. She decides to contact her pediatrician and to talk with Sara about any possible abuse. Sara denies any inappropriate touches. The following day, Sara is seen by her pediatrician, who diagnoses a yeast infection related to Sara taking antibiotics for an ear infection. He prescribes a medicated ointment. Sara's symptoms resolve and her behavior returns to normal.*

Case 3. *An 11-year-old boy, Jack, is spending a lot of time with a neighbor who goes to the same church. Jack's parents are happy that he has a friend to provide guidance because Jack has always been somewhat of a loner. The man seems to relate very well to young boys, and Jack is very attached to him, even calling him "Uncle Dave." Uncle Dave becomes a bigger part of Jack's life over time, taking him on trips, fishing, and camping. Unexpectedly, Jack changes from a quiet boy to being argumentative, loud, and always opposing his parents. He gets into fights at school and acts like he doesn't want to spend time with Uncle Dave anymore. Jack's behavior grows increasingly worse. Finally, in a calm moment, Jack's mother is able to talk to Jack about his feelings. He tells her that he feels sad sometimes and angry at other times. She is able to reassure Jack that he can tell her whatever might be happening to make him feel this way. Jack tells his mother that Uncle Dave touched his private parts. Slowly, over time, and with the supportive understanding of his parents, Jack is able to relate that for many months this man has been coercing Jack to engage in oral-genital sex and mutual masturbation. Jack admits that he was afraid to tell because he thought he wouldn't be believed and, if he was believed, he was too ashamed.*

Even though these case histories are different, they all raise concerns regarding possible sexual abuse and prompted the parents to talk with their children about possible sexually abusive experiences. In this chapter we will discuss:

🙢 ***The dynamics of sexual abuse***

🙢 ***How to talk about personal safety skills with your child***

🙢 ***The personal safety lesson***

🙢 ***What to do if you suspect your child may have been a victim of sexual abuse***

🙢 ***How to respond if your child is a victim of sexual abuse***

THE DYNAMICS OF SEXUAL ABUSE

While child sexual abuse is frightening for parents to think about, *it does happen*. In fact, given the statistics found in a number of nationwide studies, child sexual abuse is not even considered rare. One in four girls and one in six boys will be sexually victimized by the time they are 18 years old. In other words, a child is more likely to be sexually abused than suffer a broken arm or be hit by a car.

Although we as parents often warn our children about "stranger danger," about 85% of children are sexually victimized by someone they know and trust. The sexual victimization of children is an abuse of power and trust. Perpetrators can be babysitters, friends of the family, caregivers, relatives, coaches, clergy, or anyone else you regularly come into contact with. Plus, while most people think children are abused by adults, a child can also be victimized by an older child, such as a sibling, a cousin, a neighbor, or a friend.

Child sexual abuse can be defined as *any forced or tricked sexual touching of a child's or adolescent's body by an adult or an older child.* This includes:

• Fondling

• Rubbing

• Mouth-to-genital contact

• Anal or vaginal penetration

Sexual abuse also includes forcing or tricking a child into touching an adult's private parts. But sexual abuse can also occur without physical contact. Examples of this behavior include peeping, flashing, obscene phone calls, and child pornography.

Most children are tricked or manipulated, rather than forced, into sexually abusive activities, although violence can occur. Since trickery, bribery, and threats are so often a part of abuse, children are made to feel that they are to blame. As a result, they remain silent and the abuse tends to continue. While there are many reasons a child may not disclose abuse, the most frequent ones are listed in **Table 6-1.**

Child sexual abuse depends on secrecy. It is not surprising that children often believe that they are the only ones to whom this has ever happened. Children who are being abused are often not even aware that their brother or sister is also being victimized. Sometimes older children allow the abuse to continue with the belief that they are protecting their younger sibling.

While shame and fear are powerful factors in maintaining a child's silence, ignorance of personal boundaries and appropriate touching are also important factors. Confusion about what is appropriate touching by an adult versus what is too familiar, too intimate, or even violating can contribute to a child's silence or delay in telling about the abuse. This is particularly true for younger children. Often by the time a child recognizes the abusive nature of the trusted adult's behavior, he or she is beginning to experience feelings of responsibility, shame, and/or isolation—feelings that only serve to make it harder to tell. In fact, perpetrators often foster the sense of responsibility by leading the child to feel like a collaborator, saying things like:

- This is our little secret.

- This is our special way of saying goodnight.

Later in this chapter we will discuss how to help your child be more attuned to personal boundaries and to trust their own internal radar when they feel that something is not right (called that "uh-oh" feeling).

A child's safety may depend solely on his or her ability to tell about an abusive experience. **Telling is something that a child can always do, no matter what has happened.** This is an important message for a child to hear repeatedly and to learn well. Regardless of the child's ability to initially resist abusive touching, regardless of how ashamed, fearful, or responsible he may feel, the child can always tell someone about the experience. The child always has a **voice** with which to tell someone. This is one reason we emphasis to children that **their mouth is the most powerful part of their body.** Later in this chapter we will discuss how to empower your child's voice to be more effective.

Table 6-1. Reasons a Child Does Not Disclose Abuse

Feelings of shame and guilt

Fear of being in trouble or of being hurt

Fear of not being believed

Thinking that they are the only ones

HOW TO TALK ABOUT PERSONAL SAFETY SKILLS WITH YOUR CHILD

As parents, we must take the lead in providing accurate information to our children about personal safety. *Personal safety* is as important as any other kind of safety rules you teach your children. In introducing the subject of personal safety, you let your children know that you are willing to talk with them about the topic. **Do not assume that your child will ask questions about touches on their own.**

Some parents wonder if teaching their child about sexual abuse will make them curious and want to experiment with sexual touching. This has proved not to be the case. First, teaching safety rules and awareness about child sexual abuse does not require detailed descriptions of sexual acts. Just as we teach our children to look both ways before crossing the street to avoid being hit by a car without describing the gory details of what it's like to be run down, we can teach children safety rules about touching without describing sexual acts. Children need to know that this is a *potential* hazard in their lives. **Remember—an educated and informed child is a safer child.**

Parents sometimes worry that talking about touches to private parts of the body and other types of sexual abuse will frighten their children. This concern may reflect the parent's discomfort and anxiety rather than the child's. Actually, what children *imagine* sexual abuse is can often be much worse than reality. When children have been asked what they think sexual abuse is like, they often describe hideous scenarios, such as being kidnapped, taken away, and possibly killed. **Help your child replace these misconceptions with more realistic and empowering information.**

You can discuss personal safety information in the same manner you would use for other types of safety rules, such as crossing the street, playing with matches, or playing with knives. When you give your children personal safety information in a sensitive and nonthreatening way that is appropriate for his or her age and maturity level, it does not need to be intimidating or frightening for either of you. Instead, it can be a valuable tool that your children can use to protect themselves.

Talking to a child about something as important as personal safety is best done as part of a routine of open discussions with your child. You should develop the habit of having sit-down chats with your children on a regular basis. These chats can cover a lot of issues that are important to a growing child, such as:

*   Sharing

*   Honesty

*   Trust

- Friendship

- Fears

- Frustrations

- Self-respect

It is much better to explore these important topics in a comfortable, nonthreatening, fun way rather than during a time of crisis. For example, it is much easier and more effective to talk about honesty in a relaxed situation than it is after your child has been caught lying. Safety rules for all sorts of life situations can be taught and rehearsed. Such talks give your child a chance to ask questions or learn about topics that he or she might feel uncomfortable bringing up otherwise. Most importantly, these talks show that you are willing to listen to him or her and that you are open to talking about any topic—even the uncomfortable ones.

Before you sit down with your child to talk about personal safety, it is important to determine your own level of knowledge and comfort in discussing this topic. **Table 6-2** offers tips on how to prepare yourself.

When are children ready to learn about personal safety? As soon as preschool children have language skills that enable them to identify and label different parts of the body and can understand simple concepts, you can begin introducing personal safety information. You can call these **body safety rules.** For very young children, keep the information simple and concrete, such as "If someone touches your penis, you need to tell Mommy or Daddy." Since it is difficult for a young child to differentiate touches related to bathing or hygiene from sexual touches, encourage your child to tell a parent any time they are touched on the genitals. Then you will need to determine if the touch was routine care or potentially abusive.

As your child grows and his or her understanding increases, provide more information. For example, you could say, "Other people are not supposed to touch your private parts, like your

---

Table 6-2. How to Prepare Yourself to Discuss Personal Safety with Your Child

1. Review books on the subject. These are often available from your pediatrician, library, or community agencies.

2. Look for books and pamphlets written for children of different ages on this topic that you can read together with your child.

3. If you feel uncomfortable with the subject of sexual abuse or with talking with your child about private parts of the body, let your child know about your discomfort; it is likely that they will read it in your body language anyway.

4. Stress the importance of being able to discuss this awkward topic.

5. Reassure your child that he or she can talk to you about anything, no matter how embarrassing.

6. Use the appropriate terms for the private parts of the body. Remember that *vulva, penis, buttocks, rectum,* and *breasts* are just body parts, no different from knees, elbows, and noses.

---

vulva, bottom, or breasts. If someone does touch your private parts, you can say, 'No!' and then tell Mommy or Daddy right away."

It is important to discuss the following exceptions to the body safety rule:

- For young children, it is necessary for parents as well as other primary caregivers to clean the child's genital areas during diaper changes or bathing.

- If you take a child to the pediatrician, the doctor may sometimes perform a genital examination.

For young children, identifying and labeling private parts and talking about basic body safety rules may be most meaningful if it is done during bathing or dressing times. Then the child is often more aware of his or her body and more focused on the topic you are introducing. Remember to use correct terms because nicknames for these body parts can create confusion for the child and impede an adult's understanding if your child tries to communicate about inappropriate touching. Teaching your children to take care of their own toileting as soon as they are developmentally ready also makes them less vulnerable to potentially abusive experiences.

As already noted, it is difficult for parents to contemplate that their child could be a victim of abuse. In the same way, it is hard to imagine that family members, friends, or babysitters could abuse your child. However, if your child has contact with other adults and children—which every child does—then he or she may be at risk, even if you are at home full-time caring for your child. **Knowledge and a safety plan can empower your child.**

THE PERSONAL SAFETY LESSON

1. Choose a time when your child is well rested and appears receptive to talking. Also, be sure that you are not rushed.

2. Pick a place that is private and relatively free from distractions and interruptions.

3. Have available any books or other materials you may plan to use when talking to your child.

4. Use language that matches your child's age and level of understanding. If you use terms your child may not understand, explain their meaning. Also, if your child uses a word that you do not understand or that seems to be used in a different context than usual, ask him or her to define it.

5. Ask your child what he or she knows about safety, including what to do in case of fire, getting lost, or crossing the street. Also, ask if her or she knows any safety rules about personal body safety, such as different kinds of touches.

6. Help your child identify different kinds of touches. It may be helpful to use a *Touch Continuum* to discuss various touches, like the one here:

| Good Touches | Confusing Touches | Inappropriate or Hurtful Touches |

Touching ranges from good touches that a child likes, such as hugs and kisses from a parent or holding hands with a friend, to confusing touches that make a child feel confused or uncomfortable, to inappropriate or hurtful touches that a child wants to stop. Inappropriate or hurtful touches include hitting, slapping, kicking, or touches to a child's private parts. It is important that you tell your child that **sometimes people break personal safety rules and child sexual abuse happens.**

7. Encourage your child to trust his or her intuitive sense. This is the "funny feeling" that children often get when something seems wrong but they aren't sure what it is. Almost all children possess this intuitive sense. When it is encouraged and nurtured, it can be used in self-protection. As we mature, many of us lose touch with our intuitive sense, but most of us can remember when we have sensed "danger" before there was any overt indication. This ability to sense danger is unsullied in young children, who often experience it as a physical sensation. They may not talk about it much simply because they do not have the words to conceptualize it. Professionals who work in the field of child abuse prevention have come to appreciate this sense in children. The concept of the child listening to his or her "inner voice," "uh-oh feeling," or "funny feeling" is now a part of many prevention programs. Generally children can identify with the "uh-oh" feeling when an adult describes it—and you may be able to identify with it as well. You can tell the child that the "uh-oh" feeling is that funny feeling you get in your stomach when things just don't seem right. You may not be sure if something is good or bad, safe or dangerous. Prevention begins by assuring your child that these feelings exist and that they should be trusted. Often little in the child's experience tells them that these feelings are of value, so you need to validate this concept for him or her.

8. Teach your child to trust his or her sense of body space. We all have personal boundaries that mark off our body space. Depending on our relationship with a given person, the boundary changes. It may be at arm's length with a work associate, but virtually nonexistent with a loved one. Most people can sense when someone crosses into their personal space, children included.

By naming and discussing this intuitive sense of body space, you encourage children to trust their own feelings.

9. Teach your child personal body rights. Let your child know that he or she has the right to choose who touches him or her and who does not. Think about this if you find yourself insisting that your child kiss or hug a family friend or unfamiliar relative. These situations can undermine a child's belief in his or her own body rights. When you tell the child to "kiss Aunt Jane goodbye or you'll hurt her feelings," you take away the child's right to choose. Telling a child to "do what adults tell you" or permitting unwanted affection or touches from other people makes the child vulnerable to abuse. Consider asking your child how he or she would like to express respect or affection for a person. In the example of Aunt Jane, a child may feel more comfortable shaking hands or just waving goodbye.

10. Develop a safety plan with your child in case he or she receives an inappropriate touch to a private part of the body or is exposed to a sexual situation. A simple safety plan involves three actions by the child: (a) Say "No!" using an assertive or "important" voice; (b) leave as soon as you can; (c) tell a trusted adult about the experience as soon as possible. Practice this plan of action with your child, including using their "important" voice. This voice should be **strong and serious.** It should be a voice that tells the other person that your child means what he or she is saying. It doesn't have to be a yell to be effective—just make sure that it is **decisive and forceful.**

11. Help your child identify adults in his or her surroundings (home, school, neighborhood, church, synagogue) to turn to for help. Let your child know that if the first person he tells about an inappropriate or sexual touch doesn't believe it, then he should tell someone else and keep on telling until someone believes and helps.

12. Listen to your child's questions and thoughts about your discussion. Practice listening to your child even when it's uncomfortable. Show him or her that it is OK to tell you anything, even if your child may feel embarrassed or ashamed.

13. Use "what if" exercises to practice safety lessons in different situations. Then your child can practice identifying confusing or inappropriate touches or situations and can become more comfortable with thinking about the best way to handle these situations. For example:

What if you are walking home from school and someone shows you his penis? What will you do? When you get home, your parents aren't home. Who will you tell?

What if your big brother's friend likes to wrestle, but one day he starts touching your private parts? What will you do?

What if your friend tells you that her daddy is "fooling around" with her, touching her private parts and making her touch his private parts? She tells you not to tell anyone about this. What will you tell her? What will you do?

14. Talk to your child about secrets. We recommend that secrets not be kept in the family because this teaches children that it is OK to keep secrets. As an alternative, you could teach your child that secrets are not to be kept from parents. Talk to your children about the difference between a *secret* and a *surprise*. A surprise is something that is kept secret for a short time and then everyone finds out and it is fun. Secrets that are to be kept "forever" or that would make parents or other people sad are not good and are not fun. **Secrets about touches to private parts of the body are never OK and shouldn't be kept.**

Talking about personal safety with your child is an important step, but it is necessary as your child grows to periodically "check in" regarding his or her memory and understanding of personal safety rules. As your child becomes an adolescent, issues about dating and sexuality will be more easily addressed within the context of your talks about personal safety.

WHAT TO DO IF YOU SUSPECT YOUR CHILD MAY HAVE BEEN A VICTIM OF SEXUAL ABUSE

Even if you have a positive and healthy relationship with your child, he or she may be too embarrassed or scared to tell you if he or she has been sexually abused. As already discussed, there are many reasons why children may not tell.

When children do tell that they have been abused, it may be purposeful or accidental. A *purposeful* disclosure occurs when the child has made a conscious decision to tell someone. Older children are more likely to make a purposeful disclosure about their abusive experience or may tell about abuse in response to questions by a parent, teacher, or friend. Very young children are more like to *accidentally* reveal sexual victimization. Often a younger child will tell about an abusive experience out of excitement and a need to share. This is especially likely if you are talking about personal safety or if another child has talked about a similar episode. Young children often reveal possible abuse experiences through developmentally inappropriate behaviors or accidental statements. These can alert parents to possible problems. A key feature of these accidental disclosures is that neither the child nor the parents are prepared, and the result is a crisis.

You may first become aware of possible sexual abuse when you accidentally observe a child engaging in sexualized play with himself or herself, or with a toy, a pet, or another child. Your initial reaction may be shock, disbelief, or disgust. The child will interpret this as meaning that he or she has done something very wrong and will be fearful that he or she is in trouble. As a result, the child may resist engaging in further discussion or giving any explanation of how this behavior was learned or started.

Your knowledge about normal sexual development can help determine if a child's behavior is normal or needs further evaluation by a professional. Remember—young children are normally curious about their bodies as well as the bodies of others. It is not unusual for children to touch their genital areas, even to masturbate. It gives the child pleasure. However, normally the child can be instructed to touch themselves only in the privacy of his or her own bedroom. If the child has difficulty restricting this behavior or has trouble accepting your redirection, it may be necessary to investigate further. If you suddenly see the child engaging in excessive masturbation along with other changes in his or her general behavior, there may be a problem. As noted, children explore their bodies and those of their age-mates in a non-threatening, "I'll show you mine; you show me yours" fashion normally. This may occur once or twice for a child and then his or her curiosity is usually satisfied. If a child is repeatedly involved in sexual touching with a number of children, particularly if they are younger children, it may indicate a problem.

Table 6-3 outlines what to do if you observe your child engaging in sexualized behavior with another child.

Table 6-3. What to Do if Your Child is Engaging in Sexualized Behavior

- **Stay calm.**

- If the children are undressed, ask each child to get dressed in a separate area.

- Find a private place to talk to your child about what you observed.

- In a nonthreatening way, ask open-ended questions regarding where he or she learned the behavior you observed. Avoid asking leading questions and do not badger the child for answers (see Chapter 4 for help with this area).

- Talk privately with the parent(s) of the other child or children.

- Depending on the children's ages, the behavior you observed, and the information you obtain from your child, you may need to contact child protective services or the police, or your child's pediatrician.

- If you feel that your child has been involved in an abusive experience, reassure the child that he or she will be protected and make certain that you work with your pediatrician or child protective services to get *immediate* medical and psychological services, as indicated.

What might lead you to suspect that your child has been sexually abused? You may notice changes in his or her behavior, you may see physical indicators such as complaints of genital or anal discomfort, infections, or bruising of the genital area or inner thigh, or perhaps your child has told you something that makes you suspect abuse. How should you respond?

1. **Stay calm.**

2. Find a private place where you can talk without distractions or interruptions.

3. Talk about your concerns regarding your child's behaviors and/or health problems without labeling their feelings.

4. Reassure your child that he or she is not in trouble.

5. Ask your child about any worries or problems that he or she may be experiencing.

6. Allow your child time to talk about these problems or worries, even if the problems discussed are not what you were expecting or wanting to hear.

7. Listen without interruptions.

8. Do not immediately assume that your child has been sexually abused. Instead, in a matter-of-fact way, gather information by asking simple, nonleading questions.

9. If your child tells you about inappropriate sexual touch or sexual abuse, ask the nonsuggestive questions that are needed to ensure your child's immediate safety. Be sure you do not ask leading questions about particular persons or situations, such as "Who did this to you—was it Uncle Charlie?" or "Did he make you put your mouth on his penis?" Because of the legal issues involved in cases of child sexual abuse, you must avoid "contaminating" a child's statement. Parents want immediate answers regarding the possible victimization of their child—but repeated questioning or pressure to tell everything may not be in the child's best interests. In fact, a parent's repeated and intense questioning of a child can lead to misinformation because the child feels pressured to give "an answer," even if it is the wrong answer.

    a. When you are gathering information, carefully phrase your questions to avoid leading or suggesting answers to your child. Most questions that can be answered "yes" or "no" can be considered leading. Choose open-ended questions, such as "Tell me what happened." Encourage the child to tell you what happened in his or her own words.

    b. Be careful not to show shock or to blame the child. Children most often tell their story in small pieces, gauging the reaction they are seeing in the adult, usually their parent. Ironically, they often try to protect the adult from getting upset by the story. Try to listen to your child without judgment or emotional reaction. If you want to be supportive of his or her feelings, find out what they are first—do not assume that the child is angry or sad. **Ask him or her.** If children sense shock or disgust in the parent, they often first believe that it is directed at them. A parent's natural inclination is to ask, "Why didn't you tell me?" Children often interpret this question as blaming them.

10. Contact appropriate state child protective services and/or law enforcement. These agencies are mandated by law to investigate suspected child abuse and have experience in interviewing possible victims of sexual abuse.

11. Immediately seek needed medical and psychological services for your child. Children who have supportive parents or families and receive prompt, appropriate interventions have the greatest likelihood of recovering from the trauma of child sexual abuse.

> **"As a parent, your most important role after your child tells you about sexual abuse is to *believe, reassure,* and *protect* your child."**

HOW TO RESPOND IF YOUR CHILD IS A VICTIM OF SEXUAL ABUSE

As a parent, your most important role after your child tells you about sexual abuse is to **believe, reassure, and protect your child.** As discussed earlier, many children expect adults not to believe them when they tell about sexual abuse.

Important steps to take include the following:

1. Reassure your child that you are glad that he or she told you. Express some understanding of how difficult it was to tell you about the abuse. You might say, *"I believe what you're telling me and I'm glad that you told me. It took a lot of courage to talk about this."*

2. Provide support and reassure your child that the abuse was not his or her fault. Even though a child may feel responsible and to blame, sexual abuse is not the victim's fault, even if he or she couldn't say "no" to the abuse or didn't tell the parent right away. You might say, *"This was not your fault! It wasn't right and it wasn't fair for Uncle Dave to make you do that."*

3. Empower your child by letting him or her know that by telling you about the abuse, he or she has made it possible for you to do everything that you can to keep your child safe and protected

from future abuse. Let your child know that there are things that can be done to help him or her to feel better again. You might say, *"I'm glad that you told me. Now that I know I can do my best to make certain this doesn't happen again. There are some people like Child Protective Services and the police that we will need to talk to so they can help me keep you safe."* As you talk with your child, do not make promises that you can't keep. It can be unfair and damaging to make unrealistic promises, such as telling the child that you will not tell the other parent about the abuse or promising the child that he or she will not have to talk to police about the abuse.

4. Tell your child that you will need to contact appropriate child protective services and/or law enforcement officials to report the abuse. Reassure your child that he or she is not in trouble and that you will be there as a support throughout any investigation.

5. In this time of crisis, be aware that it is extremely important to rely on your own support systems, as well as professional resources to help you deal with your own feelings and the disruption to your family's life. Professionals will also be important to help you obtain information about medical, psychological, and legal services in which your child may need to be involved.

Concluding Thoughts

Every parent should know the facts about personal safety and sexual abuse that we have presented in this chapter. Unfortunately, child sexual abuse is not a rare problem. As parents, we would like to believe that it could never happen to our child--but it might. Every parent must know how to talk effectively with their children about protecting themselves from sexual abuse and about dealing with a possible abusive experience if it occurs. Remember--children can best protect themselves if they know of the potential dangers, know the options they have to deal with the problem, and know where to turn for help.

SUGGESTED READINGS

For Parents

The Safe Child Book (1985)
Sherryll Kerns Kraizer
Dell Publishing, New York, NY

Protecting Young Children from Sexual Abuse (1989)
Neil Gilbert, Jill Duerr Berrick, Nicole Le Prohn, & Nina Nyman
Lexington Books, Lexington, MA

Child Abuse Prevention Project: Manual and Guidelines (1992)
Theodore Henderson, Vicki McNeese, Joseph Kunzelman, & Raja Fattaleh
American Medical Student Association Resource Center

For Children

I Never Told Anyone (1983)
Ellen Bass & Louis Thornton
Harper & Row, New York, NY

For Kids Only: A Guide to Safety and Sexual Abuse Prevention (1993)
Catalina Herrerias
Kidsrights, Charlotte, NC

A Better Safe Than Sorry Book: A Family Guide for Sexual Assault Prevention (1984)
Sol Gordon & Judith Gordon
Prometheus Books, Fayetteville, NY

Private Zone (1982)
Frances Dayee
Warner Books, Inc., New York, NY

A Very Touching Book (1983)
Jan Hindman
Alexandria Assoc., Ontario, OR

My Body is Private (1984)
Linda Walvoord Girard
Albert Whitman & Co., Morton Grove, IL

I Told My Secret: A Book for Kids Who Were Abused (1986)
Eliana Gil
Launch Press, Walnut Grove, CA

No More Secrets for Me
Oralee Wachter
Little, Brown & Co., Boston, MA

Please Tell! A Child's Story About Sexual Abuse (1991)
Jesse
Hazelden Foundation, Minneapolis, MN

Daniel and His Therapist (1988)
Lynda Morgan
Papers Inc., Auckland, NZ

It is estimated that more than 80% of all perpetrators of child abuse and neglect are under age 40, and two-thirds are female.

Source: U.S. Department of Health and Human Services. *Child Maltreatment 1996: Reports from the States to the National Child Abuse and Neglect Data System*, Washington, D.C.: U.S. Government Printing Office, 1998.

Chapter 7

ACCUSATIONS OF ABUSE

ALLAN F. STEWART

A claim of child abuse may lead to involvement in the legal system and formal accusations. Members of the family may become involved with the legal system as a victim, as the parents of a victim, or even as an accused perpetrator. Four areas of the system may impact the family:

 The child abuse and neglect or juvenile court system–– this legal structure addresses children in need of protection or the victims of child abuse and neglect

 The criminal law system––this system deals with formal criminal indictments

 Domestic relationships law––here child custody, dissolution of marriage (divorce or annulment), or post-dissolution of marriage proceedings are handled

 Civil damages law––where persons may sue one another for wrongs; this is a growing area of legal involvement in allegations of abuse

This chapter will explore each area briefly to acquaint the family with the issues involved (see **Box 7-1** for the definition of terms used). Be aware that **whenever members of a family––whether as victim, parent, or accused—face accusations of child abuse, competent legal assistance should be sought immediately.** Names of attorneys may be obtained by contacting the State or local bar associations Family Law Section or Committee.

Box 7-1 Definition of Terms

Adjudication: The pronouncing of a judgment in a case; the determination as to the truth of the allegations of a petition.

Civil damages: A monetary award for injuries caused by another.

Disposition: The post-adjudication phase of a court proceeding where the appropriate result is determined.

Dissolution of marriage: A severing of the bonds of matrimony; formerly called divorce.

Domestic relationships: Interaction in a familial setting such as marriage or marriage-like living arrangements.

Felony: A grave offense, usually punishable by imprisonment.

Formal rules of evidence: Rules governing the presentation of facts in a court proceeding.

Guardian ad litem: The legal representative of a child.

Indictment: An accusation in writing as to the commission of an offense.

Intentional tort: A willfully done civil or private wrong.

Judicial officer: An officer administering judicial acts, such as a judge.

Judicial review: Review of actions or facts by a judicial officer.

Mandated reporter: A person designated by law who must report suspected child abuse to authorities.

Minor: An infant or person who is under the age of legal competence.

Misdemeanor: An offense of a lower grade than a felony; generally punishable by fines.

Parental rights: The rights conferred by law as aspects of being a parent, i.e., the right to custody.

Prosecuting officer: State official charged with prosecuting crimes in charges against the public, such as the states attorney or prosecuting attorney.

Recovered memory: Psychological term for remembering forgotten facts with the assistance of psychological treatment.

Statutory: Authorized or defined by state law or legislation.

Termination of rights: Legal procedure for severing the rights inherent in being a parent.

Tort: A civil wrong for which legal action may be brought.

CHILD ABUSE AND NEGLECT LEGAL SYSTEM

Each state has a statutory scheme for laws involving child abuse and neglect. The focus of these laws is to care for and protect children who are victims of child abuse and/or neglect. Included in this area is the juvenile court or family court. The juvenile court system is not designed to punish, but rather deals with the treatment and protection of victims of abuse and neglect. A parent may find himself or herself involved in the juvenile court system either as the parent of a victim or as an accused perpetrator.

Generally, child abuse or neglect allegations originate from a contact with or report from a mandated reporter, such as a school, a doctor, a hospital, or some other caregiver. Most states have laws that define who must report suspicion of child abuse and include all those persons who care for children.

The first steps that the legal system takes when an accusation of child abuse and/or neglect is made are investigation of the accusation and whatever response is needed to protect the welfare of the child. Generally the investigation is conducted by a state social worker, who is sometimes accompanied by a law enforcement officer. The purpose of the investigation is to determine if the report is valid. If the report is found to be valid, the state social investigating agency takes immediate steps to protect the child, which may include taking the child into protective custody.

Most state laws provide for a prompt review by the court of the actions leading to taking a child into protective custody. During this review, the legal system becomes involved. Both the child and the parent have the right to a timely hearing to review the appropriateness of the action. At this stage, both parent and child are entitled to representation by attorneys.

The focus of this first proceeding is not to determine whether or not child abuse or neglect took place, but rather to determine whether it is necessary to keep the child in custody for his or her own welfare. **The judicial hearing focuses on deciding if the safety of the child can be adequately assured in the child's home or if placement in an alternative environment is required.**

Regardless of whether the child remains in the home or is placed into protective custody, the matter is in the hands of the legal system at this point. Formal charges of child abuse or neglect may be made by the state prosecuting officer. Filing such charges can have far-reaching consequences for both the child and the family. **It is vital that adequate legal counsel be obtained when these formal charges are made.**

When formal charges are filed in the juvenile system, the matter enters the juvenile or family court's jurisdiction. Juvenile proceedings are divided into two aspects:

1. The adjudication phase—here the family or juvenile court must determine the truth of the allegations of child abuse and neglect. More formal rules of evidence apply, and the focus is on whether or not the evidence presented supports the allegations. If the court finds that there is not enough evidence, the involvement of the legal system may end here, although such a finding does not mean that other legal actions cannot be taken. If the court determines that there is evidence of child abuse, the case moves into the second phase.

2. The disposition process—Here the court has much greater freedom regarding the evidence that can be considered and the court orders that can be made. In the disposition phase, the court may request further evaluation of the child and family, may direct that the child should be placed in or continue in foster care or an institutional setting for the child's protection, or may return the child to the family or allow him or her to continue in the family environment with direct supervision and services provided by the state social agency.

The disposition phase of the juvenile court proceeding is often the most difficult. At all times the focus is on the child as the victim who must have his or her welfare protected. However, often protecting the child requires or results in the child being removed from his own home. In this process, the victim frequently feels even further victimized. The challenge of the disposition phase is how to adequately protect the child, treat the cause of any abuse and/or neglect, and still minimize the trauma to the child.

Most state laws and recently enacted federal legislation direct that a permanent plan for the child's protection must be developed in a timely fashion to prevent the child from spending a long time in the foster care system. If the circumstances that led to the accusations of abuse or neglect in the child's home cannot be remedied so that the child is safe, the legal system can terminate the parents' rights to the child and find the child a new home through adoption.

THE CRIMINAL LAW SYSTEM

All states have laws that make child abuse and neglect criminal offenses. The criminal charges that can be made range from serious felonies to misdemeanors, depending on the nature and the severity of the abuse or neglect. Parents and children may become involved with the criminal legal system as victims, as witnesses, or as targets of the prosecution.

The main focus of the criminal system is to punish the perpetrator of acts of child abuse and neglect. When a child or parent is the victim or witness in the prosecution of such offenders, the child's welfare must be guarded vigorously and not made secondary to the process of prosecuting and punishing the perpetrator. Most states have laws that specifically protect children in the criminal process. For example, rules that relate to the use of hearsay testimony and statements made by the child victim outside of the court may be relaxed so that such statements can be admitted into evidence through the testimony of others rather than directly by the child. This spares the child the difficult experience of testifying. In addition, many states allow the videotaping of children's testimony so that they do not have to confront the perpetrator in the stressful setting of the courtroom. Throughout the criminal process, **parents and prosecutors must remain attuned to the psychological and emotional effects these proceedings have on the child victim.**

When the parent is the accused, tremendous family upheaval may occur. The criminal legal system's primary goal of punishment may be at odds with the efforts of the juvenile and family court system's focus on treating and remedying the problem in the family. Some states allow for criminal proceedings involving family members to be transferred to the family court so that the criminal aspects can be coordinated with the family treatment process. **When the family members are both victim and accused, the parents must obtain legal assistance that is skilled in both criminal and juvenile law.** State and local bar associations may provide referral services.

> "Throughout the criminal process, parents and prosecutors must remain attuned to the psychological and emotional effects these proceedings have on the child victim."

DOMESTIC RELATIONSHIPS LAW

When accusations of child abuse arise in a family, they can lead to the breakup of the family relationship. When one parent is accused by the other of abuse of the child, either of the parents may feel compelled to dissolve the family relationship to protect the child. The law of child custody when a marriage is dissolved focuses on the interests of the child and his or her right to have a good, meaningful, and continuing relationship with each parent. The law is based on the assumption that while a man and a woman may no longer be husband and wife, they remain father and mother. In virtually all states, the standard for making custody determinations when a marriage is dissolved or when the family is already broken up remains the *best interests of the child*. Most state laws express that generally the best interests of the child are served by having the child maintain a substantial and continuing relationship with both parents. However, when accusations of abuse are made, the law focuses on protecting the child and preserving the child's best interests and welfare. According to the child's welfare needs, custody, visitation, and even contact between a parent and child can be curtailed. Alternatively, parental interactions may be supervised by appropriate persons or may even be eliminated.

The law in these situations is trying to balance the needs of the child for a continuing relationship with the parent and the protection of the child's safety and welfare. Further complications arise when the accusation of abuse is not against the parent but against a close relative of the parent. Then the extended family can become involved in the legal process.

When dealing with the clear-cut issues of serious abuse, the law's response is relatively straightforward. More difficult cases occur when the abuse takes the form of inappropriate behavior by a parent that causes discomfort for the child or places the child in the middle between two struggling parents.

Perhaps the most troubling issue in child abuse is the false accusation of abuse. This is a cruel form of abuse that comes about when one parent tries to gain an advantage over the other by implanting in the child's mind the thought that he or she has been abused by the other parent.

As in the juvenile court system, the guiding principle in child custody and domestic relationships law is to preserve and protect the child's welfare. Many states require that a separate "guardian ad litem" be appointed to represent the interests of the child when there are allegations of abuse or neglect in a domestic relations setting. The role of the guardian ad litem is to ensure that the child's rights are represented, to advocate for the child's interests, and to protect the child throughout the process. This prevents other issues involved with the dissolution of the marriage from overshadowing the welfare of the child.

CIVIL DAMAGES LAW

A new and expanding area of legal involvement in child abuse cases is the practice of civil damage or tort litigation. As more and more courts set aside the doctrine of immunity within the family, more children are taking legal actions against their parents regarding accusations of abuse. Until very recently, the doctrine of "intrafamily immunity" prevented lawsuits between members of the same nuclear family unit. However, when intentional torts or civil wrongs are involved, recent court decisions have set aside this doctrine.

This area is still controversial. Often the accusations of abuse that are presented for civil damages lawsuits date back a number of years. It is thus an adult child who is suing the parent for child abuse that occurred when the child was a minor. Issues such as the statutes of limitations complicate this field. Some courts have decided that statutes of limitations for normal civil wrongs apply directly to the actions for past abuse, whereas others hold that such statutes only begin to take effect when the adult child discovers the abuse took place.

An even more controversial aspect is the recent phenomenon identified by psychologists as "repressed" or "recovered memory." The use of hypnosis and other psychological techniques to "recover" memory of long-forgotten acts is especially troubling to the law because of questions concerning reliability and truthfulness.

Despite these difficulties involving time limitations and recovered memory, accusations of child abuse are leading to an increased number of civil damage suits. One factor that may come into play is the fact that civil action taken to address child abuse involves an intentional tort, which is not generally covered by the parent's insurance policies. Therefore any damages are the responsibility of the individual.

CONCLUDING THOUGHTS

1. *Accusations of child abuse can embroil the family in the legal system.*

2. *The first area of involvement is the traditional juvenile court or family court system.*

3. *The arena of criminal law is entered when formal criminal charges are filed.*

4. *The tragedy of families breaking up through divorce and dissolution of marriage more and more frequently involves accusations of child abuse.*

5. *The family may now be thrown into the civil damages law area when there are accusations of child abuse.*

6. *Whenever accusations of abuse or neglect are made, the members of the family must seek and obtain competent and qualified legal assistance to negotiate their way through the legal system.*

Abuse and neglect in the home causes more deaths than car accidents, fires, drowning, and other injuries.

Source: *A Nation's Shame: Fatal Child Abuse and Neglect in the United States,* April 1995, U.S. Advisory Board on Child Abuse and Neglect.

Chapter 8

CREATING A SUPPORTIVE HOME ENVIRONMENT

Karen M. Bly

Susan, choking back tears and her voice barely audible, called the Sexual Abuse clinic. As she struggled to explain the reason for her call, it was immediately evident that she was in a crisis. At 8:00 PM the prior evening, Susan had answered her door bell. The woman at her front door introduced herself as a Department of Family Services hotline investigator who was there to investigate an allegation of sexual abuse involving Susan's 7-year-old son as the victim. Susan described her total unawareness, disbelief, and shock regarding the allegation. In fact, she actually thought she was dreaming the entire scenario of the hotline investigator's visit. Susan expected to awaken at any moment to discover that none of this was real; it had to be a nightmare!

The hotline investigation, however, was a reality. As the story unfolded, Susan learned that her son, Ray, had told his teacher about the abuse. Apparently, the husband of Ray's babysitter had fondled Ray several times. Two days before the hotline was notified, the babysitter's husband tried to persuade Ray to masturbate him and to perform oral sex on him. The next day, after a classroom discussion on "good touch–bad touch," Ray disclosed the incidents to his teacher. As a mandated reporter, the teacher appropriately followed her school protocol, and the disclosure was reported to the hotline. Unfortunately, the school was unable to contact Susan and her husband before the hotline investigator arrived at their home.

Once interviewed, it was evident to the investigator and Ray's parents that inappropriate sexual contact had occurred. Susan was devastated; she blamed herself for not realizing her son had been victimized. Distraught, Susan called the Sexual Abuse clinic (Special Assessment and Management or SAM clinic) with her crisis-generated questions:

Why didn't Ray tell her what was happening at the babysitter's home?

What could she do in the future to encourage Ray to talk to her about problems?

Did this mean she was a bad mother?

How could she provide a home environment that would enable her son to trust her with his concerns?

Parents must be willing to talk to their children about physical and sexual abuse. Teaching your child to protect himself is a priority. It not only allows you to provide the child with the information needed to feel in charge of his or her own body, but it also may enable a child to disclose existing abuse.

As parents, you may be uncomfortable talking about abuse with your child. It is important to realize that such discussion is as important as teaching the child to wash his or her hands. You may fear that you will scare the child with the "unnecessary" information. As discussed in Chapter 6, you can consider approaching the discussion as you would if you were teaching your child general hygiene and safety rules. The information is essential if the child is going to be able to protect herself. By taking this approach of discussing abuse with the child as part of his or her ongoing health and safety training, the child will benefit from the repetition. The information will be accepted as a routine learning topic rather than as a terror-provoking "lecture." Although dramatically phrased, in the "war" against abuse, children must be armed with the ammunition to prevent the invasion of and damage to their bodies.

Each day parents call seeking help for their concerns regarding the possible or actual abuse of their child. Their phone call may simply be a means of obtaining information about the indicators of physical or sexual abuse. Frequently, however, they call to inform the sexual abuse team that their child has disclosed abuse and to be instructed in what to do next. Parents often feel responsible and guilty that they didn't recognize the warning signs sooner. It is so easy once we know what has happened to ruminate over the pieces of the puzzle that were at first overlooked, but now seem so obvious. **Do not waste valuable time grieving about what was missed or never even noticed in the past.** Instead, focus on the present situation and plan for the future. What has already occurred cannot be changed. Whatever may be occurring currently can be stopped. And, most importantly, whatever abuse that may occur in the future can be prevented.

For the parents who value their child and the child's quality of life, a supportive home environment is essential. What is meant by the vague term "supportive home environment?" Such a climate would not only allow a child to disclose his or her feelings and concerns openly, but it would also encourage the child to do so. Such an environment is based on an atmosphere of mutual trust and respect. Trust and respect develop from a solid foundation of honesty and openness shared between parent and child. Blaming and accusations are not part of this foundation. The key to all of this is **communication.** And communication is more than just talking, teaching, and explaining. To be really effective, communication must include listening.

Communication occurs in many forms. One mother expressed the importance of communication when she innocently and simply stated, "I've gone over good touch and bad touch with her since she was in my womb." One of the most eloquent examples of the value of communication and a supportive home environment was provided by the parent of a young boy who had recently disclosed sexual abuse. The boy's mother offered the following thoughts and advice to share with other parents:

Do you talk to your children?

Do you listen to your children?

I never thought it would happen to my child.

You can never say it enough to your child. How can I tell everyone in the world what to look for?

You have to talk to your children and let them know what's out there.

You need to get information and approach it in the right way with your children.

You may not want to deal with it, but you have to.

> "What has already occurred cannot be changed. Whatever may be occurring currently can be stopped. And, most importantly, whatever abuse that may occur in the future can be prevented."

The pain this mother was feeling is evident. She obviously respects the critical importance of communicating with your child. Significantly, she is also planning for the future and the valuable opportunities to help her child prevent and/or avoid future abuse.

APPROACHES TO CREATING A SUPPORTIVE HOME ENVIRONMENT

Parents often ask, "How should I approach my child if I suspect he or she has been abused?" The response involves three key guidelines:

1. *Listen* to what your child says.

2. *Clarify* what your child has said. Ask only open-ended questions. For example, if the child says, "Daddy hurt me," ask "How did Daddy hurt you?" If the child says, "Uncle Johnny touched my pee-pee," ask, "What did Uncle Johnny touch your pee-pee with?"

3. *Do not ask direct questions.* In other words, do not ask the child "Did Uncle Johnny touch your pee-pee with his penis?" Also, do not ask "Did Uncle Johnny put his finger in your pee-pee?" These are leading questions and can be misinterpreted as an attempt or intent to coach the child.

If you suspect that your child has been abused, use the three key guidelines just noted and then decide if you want to use the direct or the indirect approach. An acronym for the indirect approach is **TAPS:**

T   **Teach**

A   **About**

P   **Private parts of the body and**

S   **Safe touch**

Teaching can be done at home or more formally as part of a school education program. This involves teaching the child about *private parts* of his or her body (that is, the parts covered by a swimming suit) and about general body *safety.* The teaching should be offered on the child's level of understanding and must use words that child is familiar with. We highly recommend using correct anatomical terms such as "penis" and "vagina." However, since many children (and parents) seem more comfortable with the term "private parts," it is okay to use that term.

During formal and informal teaching sessions, a child may feel safe and comfortable with the topic and may disclose current or past abuse. This disclosure may be so spontaneous and unexpected that you may be unprepared for what the child is revealing. However, many children do not disclose abuse spontaneously. Thus, during the teaching/discussion session about abuse, you may ask the child "Has anyone ever made you feel uncomfortable?" By including this as part of the discussion, you have provided the child with an appropriate opportunity to disclose.

Be sure to reinforce to the child the importance of telling someone whether it be a parent, teacher, relative, or adult friend, if anything has occurred that has made him or her uncomfortable or if there is anything that he or she is concerned about.

The acronym **LACE** can be used for the direct approach to abuse:

L   **Listen**

A   **Ask (carefully!)**

C   **Clarify**

E   **Empower your child and yourself and Express concern**

You must *listen* to your child. Probably something the child has already said or done has raised your suspicion that the child may have been victimized. When *asking* about your suspicion, remember the key guideline: Use only indirect questions to *clarify*. **Do not ask the child if the specific person you suspect has abused him or her.** However, share your general concern with the child. For example, you might say, "I've noticed for several weeks that you are afraid to go to the babysitter's house. What can I do to make you feel better?" Or, if you notice suspicious bruises on the child, you might ask, "What caused these marks on your legs?" This is more acceptable than asking "Did the babysitter hit you?" Most importantly, *empower* your child and yourself. The child who discloses abuse can, in many situations, be protected. The child who has learned what is appropriate and inappropriate touch also knows that he or she must tell someone when touched inappropriately or hurt. When you assume the responsibility for teaching the child, you empower the child with the ability to protect himself or herself.

SPECIFIC TOOLS FOR CREATING A SUPPORTIVE HOME ENVIRONMENT

An acronym that summarizes and emphasizes the necessary ingredients for providing a supportive home environment is **GOALS FOR PARENT AND CHILD.**

GOALS. The "G" represents *genitalia* and is mentioned here to restate the recommendation that you teach your child the correct anatomical terms for body parts. An experienced professional would never interview or counsel a child without first establishing the words the child uses to represent body parts, including genitalia. This is essential to avoid misinterpretation of what the child is disclosing.

The "O" represents *open discussion of problems, concerns, and sexuality.* Isn't it better if the child learns about sex and sexuality from his or her parents rather than from peers, who may provide inaccurate information? If the child can participate at home in open discussions, then it follows that the child may feel comfortable to discuss any personal problems or concerns.

The "A" represents *allowing the child to talk and express his or her feelings.* Encourage the child to come to you with problems. This means that you will *listen* ("L") to your child. If the child has something to share with you, you must allow the time he or she needs to discuss this and listen without interruption as necessary.

The "S" represents several ideas, including *solve the problem, seek help in dealing with the problem,* and *support the child emotionally through the crisis.* Be advised, however, that if abuse is occurring, solving the problem is going to be a very involved process and will not occur immediately.

FOR. The "F" reminds you to provide *fun* and humor for the child and family even in the midst of the crisis. Continue to live! Find joy and pleasure in taking walks, watching cartoons together, or just playing with the family dog. Continue to laugh together as well as share tears.

The "O" emphasizes the importance of using the *opportunities to protect, love, teach, understand, and support your child.*

The "R" recalls the value of maintaining *realistic expectations.* Rome wasn't built in a day; the movie *Jurassic Park* took months of planning and filming; and even planning a vacation requires an investment of time. Therefore do not expect your child to immediately and spontaneously disclose his or her "secret." Instead, accept that this may take time. If abuse has occurred and an investigation follows, this, too, will take time. If your child has behavior problems as a result of abuse, accept that these will require time and patience for resolution. In fact, do not expect justice, or you may be very disappointed and frustrated.

PARENT. "P" represents the *priorities of providing privacy and protection.* Privacy means that only those who have a "need to know" about the disclosed situation or your concerns actually need to know. Protection is self-explanatory–protect the child from the alleged perpetrator of the abuse.

The "A" represents several issues, the main one being *avoid.* Things to avoid include *anger, accusations, annoyance,* or *anxious responses* to your child. This means you must be aware of your feelings and how you are reacting.

For the "R," *respond calmly,* but do *respond* to your child. Along with this, the "E" represents *emotions.* You must control your emotions as much as is reasonably possible. An emotional response is normal, but emotions should not be allowed to run rampant. Your child has possibly been through an experience in which he or she had no control; he or she will depend on you to take control and model self-restraint for him or her.

The "N" highlights the importance of a *nonjudgmental* atmosphere. This is essential if you want to encourage your child to talk to you and share with you.

The meaning of "T" is probably obvious by now. *Talk* with your child and allow time for your child to talk to you.

AND. "A" represents the importance of establishing an *atmosphere of acceptance.* Let the child know you are his or her advocate. Being your child's advocate is a priority; the child is relying on you.

"N" encourages you to *neutralize the crisis* (if one exists) and provide *normalcy* for the child.

The "D" is a reminder to *decide* what needs to be done; *demonstrate* understanding; and be *dependable.*

CHILD. If I had to choose the one most valuable tip for parents in creating a supportive home environment, it would be *communicate.* I will elaborate further in a moment.

The next letter, "H," represents several different ideas and thoughts. *Honesty* with your child and with yourself is essential. Help the child *heal* emotionally. If a child has been abused, there are always some emotional wounds. Above all, do not give up *hope.* You may not realize the ultimate outcome you desire, but the situation will probably improve.

Improvement occurs only with *intervention;* thus the "I" is explained. Intervention may be accomplished by professional child protection workers, counselors, the legal system, or the empowered parent or child.

The "L" highlights a basic concept of great importance: *Learn* the signs and symptoms of abuse; *learn* prevention strategies; *learn* anger control; and *learn* how to communicate with your child.

Finally, the "D" represents *don't be disappointed* with your child. Regardless of what has happened, you must remember that it was not his or her fault.

SUGGESTIONS FOR COMMUNICATION SKILLS WITH YOUR CHILD

In responding to your child, be aware of your behavior, both verbal and nonverbal. If you are silent and say nothing, this may be interpreted by the child as a warning that you are unwilling or unable to discuss the issue. As a result, the child may quit his initial and all future attempts to discuss problems with you. If you are uncomfortable discussing an issue or situation, be honest about this with your child. Children are very perceptive and are often quite aware of parental discomfort with an issue. Acknowledging your discomfort helps to establish an atmosphere of honesty. Honesty usually strengthens the development of trust.

Your body language may inadvertently convey the message that the topic is taboo. Maintaining a physical distance from your child, avoiding eye contact with your child, or just having a look on your face may be keys that turn off the discussion. Have you ever had the opportunity to watch a videotape of yourself? If you have, think about the gestures and facial expressions you made that you were previously unaware of. Then think about the message this body language may give a frightened or upset child. Remember also that the tension in your voice may be misinterpreted by the child, who may see it as disappointment, disbelief, or anger toward him or her. Reassure your child that these feelings are not directed at him or her. If you are upset, angry, or even embarrassed during the discussion, share these feelings honestly with your child. At the same time, reinforce with your child the promise that you will listen to him or her and reassure the child that what he or she has to say is important to you.

What you say is also important. Responding with, "Uncle Johnny didn't mean to make you feel uncomfortable when he kissed you on the lips" minimizes and negates your child's feelings. If an act made your child feel uncomfortable, acknowledge that the act indeed was inappropriate. Encourage your child to trust his or her "gut" reaction to a situation and to respond accordingly.

Allow your child to ask questions and to clarify any confusion he or she has regarding the situation. If your child is afraid, reassure him or her that you are there as his or her advocate.

Specific Suggestions and Counseling

Try to maintain a normal daily routine for your child. This includes consistency in family rules, setting limits, routine discipline, school, and entertainment. And don't forget those trips to the mall or to a movie.

Creating a supportive home environment may also require seeking professional counseling as follow-up care for both you and your child. Disclosure of any kind of abuse—whether physical, emotional, or sexual—creates stress for the entire family. Although the disclosure may not reveal an emergency situation, it certainly creates a crisis because of the importance of the matter and its impact on the family. As a parent, accept the fact that you and your child may need to seek professional help to deal with the situation.

You may feel overwhelmed by confusion and emotions associated with the disclosed situation. Remind yourself that such a reaction is *normal.* Identify a friend, relative, coworker, or significant other whom you trust and with whom you can share your feelings. Allow yourself to seek out this person as your emotional support system. Follow the cliché—*take one day at a time.* Don't expect immediate results. Healing takes time, but time does allow for healing. The term *crisis* by definition means the situation is short lived. Eventually, normalcy can reappear in your lives. Complete recovery may depend on the previously mentioned professional counseling. Your child's pediatrician, local child protection agency, or a mental health facility will be able to provide you with appropriate referrals.

SUGGESTED READINGS

American Academy of Pediatrics. (1991). Guidelines for the evaluation of sexual abuse of children. *Pediatrics* 87:254-259.

Botash A. (1994). What office-based pediatricians need to know about sexual abuse. *Contemporary Pediatrics* 2:83-100.

Channing L. Bete Co., Inc. (1992). *About preventing child abuse.* (Brochure). South Deerfield, MA.

Channing L. Bete Co., Inc. (1994). *About sexual victimization of children.* (Brochure). South Deerfield, MA.

Channing L. Bete Co., Inc. (1995). *What everyone should know about the sexual abuse of children.* (Brochure). South Deerfield, MA.

Channing L. Bete Co., Inc. (1995). *Anger and how to handle it.* (Brochure). South Deerfield, MA.

Channing L. Bete Co., Inc. (1995). *The hidden hurt—child sexual abuse.* (Brochure). South Deerfield, MA.

Hymel K, and Jenny C. (1996). Child sexual abuse. *Pediatrics in Review* 17:236-249.

Krugman R. (1986). Recognition of sexual abuse in children. *Pediatrics in Review* 8:25-30.

Myers J. (1994). Evaluation and treatment—Can we believe what children say about sexual abuse? *The APSAC Advisor* 7:5-6.

Williams J. (1996). The cycle of abuse. In J. Monteleone (ed). *Recognition of child abuse for the mandated reporter* (pp. 147-159). St. Louis, MO: GW Medical Publishing, Inc.

Since 1990, 10,000 American children have died at the hands of their parents or caretakers.

Source: *A Nation's Shame: Fatal Child Abuse and Neglect in the United States*, April 1995, U.S. Advisory Board on Child Abuse and Neglect.

CHOOSING CAREGIVERS FOR YOUR CHILD

Peggy S. Pearl, Ed. D.

We as parents can find ourselves in situations that require a surrogate parent or caregiver for various reasons. Regardless of the circumstance, how to go about selecting a caregiver is very important and can have life-long impact on the child. Don't feel overwhelmed by the decision's importance or complexity, though. By developing a plan of action that matches the community's resources with your values and needs, the outcome can be a great choice.

Collecting Relevant Information

Once you decide that a caregiver is required, your first step is to collect relevant information. Research has shown that making child care arrangements that are consistent from day to day is important to your child's security and readiness for school. The National Association for the Education of Young Children says children fare better emotionally, socially, and cognitively when child care centers or family child care homes demonstrate the following:

- Sufficient staffing, which refers to the number of adults for each child. Optimally, you want high staff-to-child ratios.

- Smaller group sizes—not too many children grouped together.

- Higher levels of staff education and specialized training.

- Low staff turnover and stability among the administration of the care facility.

- Higher levels of staff compensation.

The decision-making process involved with choosing child care will require time and effort on your part. Most families choose care that is either a "family child care home" or "child care center" rather than a "caregiver" who comes into their home.

- Family child care homes may mean leaving the child with a family member or friend, or it may mean using a family-operated business. Usually, these providers care for fewer than 8 to 10 children in their own home. Some family child care homes have an assistant caregiver during all or part of the day.

- Child care centers provide care for groups of children in a facility specially designed for child care. The maximum number of children per each group is determined by child care licensing based on the age of the child.

- Child care in your own home is considerably more expensive and more difficult to find.

Since out-of-home care is more common, its selection process will be discussed first.

Out-of-Home Care

You will need to use community support services to learn about the child care options in your community. Talk to your family, friends, and co-workers for possible child caregivers. Your church may also be a good source of information. But don't stop there! You should consult the Resource and Referral Agencies (R & R) in your community. These agencies have a complete listing of available child care in your community. The database includes the name and location of programs, the hours of operation, cost, ages of children cared for, slots available, and other services such as transportation to and from school. Available free or for a small fee, an R & R provides parents with a list of child care options. The list will quickly help you determine what your options are. If your community does not have an R & R, check the business listings of the phone book, your employer's human resources office, and the local child care licensing office. Before looking at all of the listings, it is best to decide if you prefer a family child care home or a child care center.

Licensing. The licensing process for child care providers requires a complete investigation of the child care facility. This includes an inspection of the physical premises of the facility, a review of the qualifications of staff, and an inspection of other records that must be kept on file in the facility. When licensing requirements are met, you have the assurance that minimum standards are met regarding nutrition, daily activities, and the health and safety of your children. Licensing staff also provide consultation services to child care providers in an effort to encourage and support quality child care.

Be aware that states vary in the specific laws and regulations regarding child care. The child care licensing office will be listed in the telephone directory. This consumer service is part of the state child protective services in 48 states, and it is in the state department of health in Kansas and Missouri. Be sure to:

- Ask the local child care licensing office for a list of licensed facilities.

- Obtain and read a copy of the licensing rules.

- Read the records of each program you are considering. The licensing records are open to the public and very informative to parents.

Note that the licensing process provides safety assurance for consumers. Just as with the licensing of restaurants, beauty shops, and hospitals, it assures that basic health and safety standards are met. Most states also require a planned curriculum appropriate to the age of the child, adequate safe equipment and materials, and in-service training for the staff. The structural safety of the building, water quality and temperature, safety of heating and cooling systems, appropriate fire exits, etc. are checked by either the licensing staff or other trained professionals. Any food that is served must be prepared and stored under sanitary conditions and meet the U.S. Department of Agriculture nutrition recommendations. Remember—licensing assures *minimum* standards are met. The *quality* of a program, however, is an accreditation issue.

Accreditation. Accreditation is a "stamp of approval" designed to promote quality programs both in licensed child care homes and in child care centers for young children, birth through age 13 years. Accreditation gives recognition to child care providers who meet certain indicators of quality. Programs that meet quality standards are accredited by the National Association for the Education of Young Children [800 424-2460] (or the Missouri Accreditation for Early Childhood and School-age Programs [573 876-2321]), or the National Association for Family Day Care [515 282-8192]. The decision to seek accreditation demonstrates the caregiver's desire for a quality program. The standards are developed by professionals in early childhood care and education. The standards for both homes and centers address appropriate practices in the following areas:

- Health and safety of the environment

- Building self-esteem in each child

- Providing positive guidance

- Providing for positive interactions between children and adults

- Effective home and child care program coordination

- Creative development

- Language development and pre-reading and reading skills

- Physical and intellectual growth and development

- Social and emotional growth and development

- Staff formal education and specialized early childhood training

- Effective staff communication

- Effective management practices

Look for the licensing and accreditation certificates. Both of these should be posted.

PROGRAM COMPARISON PROCESS

Now that you have collected the relevant information about child care, the second step in your plan is to compare programs as they relate to your list of expectations, which you should be developing throughout the information collection process. The program comparison step requires your personal involvement in visiting the various programs.

Visiting Programs

It is usually best to call and verify the information you have about all of the programs you are considering. When you talk to the program director or care provider, ask if you may come to visit anytime or if you need an appointment. If you have the freedom to choose, plan to visit a prospective program at different times of the day during different types of activities. When you visit, notice if you feel welcome and if you are encouraged to come back.

Ask questions. During the visit, you should seek answers to the following questions:

- How does the center or home look? Sound? Smell? Feel?

- What is the noise level? Excessive noise is a sign of lack of planning and a source of stress and distraction to both adults and children.

- Are children busy learning as they play? Is there a pleasant hum of activity rather than silence dominated by a teacher's voice? Or is there uncontrolled noise?

- Is the environment free of clutter and confusion, but "used" by the children? Or is it "too" clean and orderly? Do children make free choices between a variety of planned learning centers?

- How does the playground look? Feel? Is it free of clutter?

Observe. While listening carefully to the answers, you should observe whether the program "practices what they preach." For example, ask what the program goals are for the children. Does the answer match your goals for your child? Ask how the program individualizes the curriculum so everybody learns. Listen for open-ended situations that encourage children to choose between two or three activities, to ask questions, and to explore interesting topics. Children should not be expected to all be doing the same things at the same time except, of course, during mealtime and naptime.

You should also ask how the program personnel define reading and writing for preschoolers. Listen for a broad, inclusive answer such as *"pretending to read a book or scribbling 'letters' are important pre-reading and writing activities for preschoolers. Listening and asking questions about what someone reads to them encourages children to read and write. School-aged children should be encouraged to read as well as write their own books."*

Tables 9-1 and **9-2** list some of the questions you should ask during the decision-making process. These check lists are designed to help you decide what things about child care arrangements are most important to you and your family. They can also help you make sure your child's arrangement offers the things you believe are important. Note that not everything will apply to your family's situation.

Other Considerations

The answers to your questions will supply additional information to assist you in making an informed decision. Your notes about several child care centers or family child care homes will help you in making your final decision. With all the information you have collected, you need to consider these questions:

- How much can you afford to pay?

- What hours is care available, and how is care provided after hours if you arrive late to pick up your child?

- Where is the care located?

- Where will your child be the safest and healthiest?

- Who do you feel will give your child the best care?

- Which caregiver offers the activities that your child will enjoy most and derive the greatest benefit from?

Trust your judgment. The information you gathered, your knowledge of your child, your own child-rearing practices, and your personal judgment about people will all help you make the best decision. You know your child better than anyone else. By going through this process, you will make the best choice available to you.

Table 9-1. Questions to Ask When Choosing Child Care

DOES THE CAREGIVER . . .	YES	NO
Appear to be warm and friendly?	___	___
Seem calm and gentle?	___	___
Seem to have an appropriate sense of humor?	___	___
Seem to be someone with whom you can develop a relaxed, sharing relationship?	___	___
Seem to be someone your child will enjoy being with?	___	___
Seem to feel good about herself or himself and her or his job?	___	___
Have child-rearing attitudes and methods that are similar to your own?	___	___
Consistently use positive language in stating expectations or when guiding behaviors rather than lots of NOs and "stop thats"?	___	___
Never threaten, shame, or ridicule when correcting children's behavior?	___	___
Treat each child as a special person?	___	___
Understand what children can and want to do at different stages of development?	___	___
Have the right materials and equipment on hand to help the child learn and grow mentally and physically?	___	___
Patiently help children solve their own problems?	___	___
Provide activities that encourage children to think and talk things through?	___	___
Encourage good health habits such as washing hands throughout the day?	___	___
Provide appropriate outdoor experiences each day, except in very harsh weather?	___	___
Talk to the children and encourage them to express themselves through words?	___	___
Encourage children to express themselves in creative ways?	___	___
Have art, movement, and music activities suited to the ages of all children in care?	___	___

Table 9-1. Questions to Ask When Choosing Child Care, *con't.*

DOES THE CAREGIVER . . .	YES	NO
Seem to have enough time to supervise all the children in his or her care?	___	___
Help each child to know, accept, and feel good about himself or herself?	___	___
Help each child become independent in ways you approve?	___	___
Help your child learn to get along with and to respect other people, no matter what their appearance, background, or behaviors are?	___	___
Accept and respect your family's cultural values?	___	___
Provide a routine and rules the children can understand and follow?	___	___
Take time to discuss your child with you regularly?	___	___
Allow each child to do things for himself or herself because he or she understands everyone learns from mistakes?	___	___
Help each child increase his or her vocabulary by talking with him or her, listening, reading aloud, and answering questions?	___	___
Accept and respect all children, regardless of ability or special needs?	___	___
Have previous experience and education in working with children in a group setting?	___	___

IF YOU HAVE AN INFANT OR TODDLER (BIRTH TO AGE 3) . . .

	YES	NO
Seem to enjoy cuddling your baby?	___	___
Spend time holding, playing with, and talking to each baby?	___	___
Look each child in the eye when talking to, feeding, and diapering?	___	___
Provide stimulation by pointing out things to look at, touch, and listen to?	___	___
Cooperate with your efforts to toilet train your toddler?	___	___

Table 9-1. Questions to Ask When Choosing Child Care, *con't.*

DOES THE CAREGIVER . . .	YES	NO
Realize that toddlers want to do things for themselves and help each child to learn to feed and dress himself or herself, go to the bathroom, and pick up his or her own toys?	___	___
Help each child learn language by talking with him or her, naming things, reading aloud, describing what he or she is doing, and responding to each child's words?	___	___

IF YOUR CHILD IS SCHOOL-AGED (6 TO 14 years) . . .

	YES	NO
Give each child supervision and security, but also understand his or her growing need for independence?	___	___
Set reasonable and consistent limits?	___	___
At the same time allow each child to make choices and gradually take responsibility?	___	___
Teach nonviolent conflict resolution techniques for all children to use with peers?	___	___
Understand the development of children 6 to 14 years of age?	___	___
Help each child follow through on projects, help with homework, and suggest interesting things to do?	___	___
Encourage literacy skills with writing, reading, public speaking, and dramatic activities?	___	___
Listen to each child's problems and experiences?	___	___
Respect each child when he or she expresses new ideas, values, or opinions?	___	___
Cooperate with all parents to set clear limits and expectations about behaviors?	___	___
Understands the conflicts and confusion older school-aged children feel about sex, identity, and pressure to conform?	___	___
Provide your child with a good adult role-model to admire and copy?	___	___

Table 9-2. Does the Day Care Center or Home Have . . .

	YES	NO
An up-to-date license?	___	___
A current accreditation by the National Association for the Education of Young Children (or in Missouri the Accreditation for Early Childhood and School-age Programs)?	___	___
Enough space indoors (minimum 35 square feet/child) and outdoors (minimum 75 square feet/child) so all the children can move freely and safely?	___	___
Knowledgeable staff, educated in child growth and development as well as techniques for working with children in a group setting?	___	___
Low adult-child ratios and smaller group sizes?	___	___

Birth to 2 years	1 adult to 4 children, no more than 8
2-year-olds	1 adult to 8 children, no more than 16
4- to 6-year-olds	1 adult to 12 children, no more than 24
School-aged children	1 adult to 16 children, no more than 32

	YES	NO
A low staff turnover and administrative stability?	___	___
An open environment where no adult is ever totally alone with a child and out of the sight of other adults?	___	___
Parent handbooks to outline services provided, policies, ill children, and expectations of the parents?	___	___
Written discipline policy distributed to all parents and known and followed by all staff members?	___	___
A discipline policy forbidding corporal punishment?	___	___
Written policy for the transfer of responsibility of children from parent to staff at the beginning of the day and for transfer at the end of the day?	___	___
Written policy on who may pick each child up from the center or home?	___	___
Regular rest periods for staff, away from children?	___	___
Written accident reports on file?	___	___
Written procedures for dealing with suspected abuse of children by staff?	___	___
Emphasis on managing the environment, not on managing the children?	___	___

INVOLVEMENT AND FOLLOW-UP PROCESS

Once you have made your decision, continue the business transaction. Ask for a written agreement that states:

- Cost

- What will be done in emergencies

- Daily routine

- Days and hours care will be given

- Caregiver's responsibilities

- Your responsibilities as parent

Most programs have a parent handbook, and some have a legal contract that both you and the caregiver will sign.

Stay Involved

You need to continuously observe your child's caregiver, the home or center, as well as your child's behavior. Get to know the caregiver and observe the interactions that take place in the group or home. Ask your child about activities and new friends. Listen to your child's comments. Listen to the language that caregivers use with your child. Verbal abuse is serious, and the consequences may last longer than those of physical abuse. **Ridicule, threats, and shaming should never be used with children of any age.**

Continue to drop by the child care center or family child care home at different times of the day. Your presence will make your child feel good and you can gain reassurance that you made a good child care decision. Be suspicious if the center has rules limiting when you can visit your child and where in the facility you may go. The program should share a list of parents with addresses and phone numbers. Get to know other parents of children enrolled in the program. If there is a parent group, participate.

Do not give permission for "spanking" or other discipline that you do not approve of or use. The combination of overly stressed or tired caregivers and corporal punishment can open the possibility of physical abuse. Only give permission for planned field trips and only sign a release for one day's outing—not a blanket approval for any field trip. *(Be realistic; that doesn't mean children and caregiver couldn't decide to walk around the block to look at the leaves.)* If you have chosen a family home provider, consult with him or her about when children will be routinely taken out of the home.

As you use your child care program, continue to mentally compare the practices you observe with the licensing rules you read during the decision-making process. Do you notice any practices or policies of the program that do not conform to the licensing rules? Discuss any repeated discrepancies with the director. If you are not satisfied with the response you get, or if you see no change, call the child care licensing agency.

Be sensitive to any changes in your child's behaviors. Overly passive or aggressive behavior, ripped, torn or missing clothes, bruises, or other physical marks may be signs of neglect or abuse—or just the result of the child's play. Ask for an explanation from your child and the caregiver. Do the answers match? Assure your child that he or she did nothing wrong—**DON'T punish or blame your child.** Talk with other parents. Listen to what your child(ren) says about their caregivers as well as what they say about other children. When a child tells you he or she does not want to be with someone, there may be a good reason why. **If your children tell you about touching, or any other sexual behavior by an adult, believe them.** Children do not make up stories about sexual abuse. Preschool children cannot make up stories when they have not had any first-hand experience with that activity. School-aged children rarely make up stories about sexual touching. Take your child seriously and call child protective services if you suspect your child has been mistreated in any way. **However, remember child abuse in child care is rare.**

> **"If your children tell you about touching, or any other sexual behavior by an adult, believe them."**

Most importantly, have a positive attitude about your choice. If you feel good about your child care arrangement, usually your child will, too, and everyone will have a better day.

Choosing In-home Child Caregivers

In-home caregivers are the best option for some families. The child is allowed to stay in his or her own home. You may want to use in-home care if your child has special needs because of a physical, mental, or emotional problem. If you need care for an infant or toddler or care for a child at night, or if you are looking for long and/or irregular hours, in-home care may be best. The main disadvantages of in-home care are finding the best fit of caregiver and family and costs. You may choose a placement service to screen applicants and give you the names of individuals to interview. They will be expected to do a background check before you are given the names. A background check, regardless of who does it, should include a child protective services and law enforcement check for child maltreatment and any other felony conviction. Be sure to call all references that are given. Ask specific questions relating to the

individual's ability to care for children. Suggested reference questions are listed in **Table 9-3.** Notice that there are no right or wrong responses to these questions when you are merely gathering data on which to make a decision. Also note that written, non-confidential references are not appropriate because they are seldom objective. Always require confidential written references. When requesting college transcripts, always require an official copy directly from the college or university. Remember that even though all of this is time consuming, what you are doing is very important to expose any misrepresentation of previous experience.

Individuals who say that their greatest asset as a caregiver is their patience may not be the best choice. Patience has a limit. Better traits are knowledge of child growth and development as well as demonstrated skills in nurturing children. An important part of nurturing is unconditional acceptance of the child and providing guidance for him or her in positive behaviors. By understanding normal growth and development, caregivers anticipate what children are capable of doing and their normal fears, frustrations, and behaviors. This knowledge allows them to plan and anticipate to avoid many situations that could cause problems.

As with any business agreement, you need a formal written agreement. A written job description and personnel policy discussed in detail before employment begins will prevent later problems. Be specific about pay, hours of employment, vacation, emergency illnesses, sick leave, personal business days, meals, transportation, and any other special considerations, such as smoking policy or type of dress required. Making a list of specific "house rules" may prevent misunderstanding as the relationship develops. Include the child(ren) in preparing the "house rules" to ensure that the child knows the mutually agreed upon expectations. Written messages to verify verbal messages may facilitate communication.

CHOOSING PART-TIME CAREGIVERS

Choosing a babysitter for the evening or day is also important, and you should review the previous discussions to see parts that apply. Some of the interview questions are listed in **Table 9-3.** If you do not know the individual personally, requesting references and a background check is appropriate. Using **Table 9-4,** check references carefully. Once you have made a decision, be aware that even though the arrangement is less formal, a written list of house rules left where they are readily available has advantages.

Table 9-3. Possible Interview Questions

- What activities would you expect a child 6 years old [the age(s) of your child(ren)] to enjoy?

- What do you enjoy doing outdoors with children?

- What type of discipline did your parents use with you when you were young? How effective was it? What were you disciplined for?

- How do you think children learn? Give an example of how you would set up a learning experience for a child.

- How would you settle a dispute between 2-year-olds who want the same toy at the same time? Two 5-year-olds?

- What would you plan to feed a 6-year-old (or the age of your child) child during a day?

- If a parent, what type of discipline did you use with your children? When do you remember using discipline, and in what situations?

- What are your personality traits that you consider assets as a caregiver?

- How would you describe your own childhood?

- What are your interests or hobbies?

Table 9-4. Sample Questions for References

- In what capacity did you know this individual?

- How would you describe the applicant's strengths and weaknesses in working with young children?

- Give an example of how this individual avoided problem behavior by anticipating and redirecting.

- How would you describe the applicant's philosophy of working with young children and their family?

- How would you describe the applicant's relationships with adults?

- Would you hire or rehire this individual if you had a position available? Why?

CONCLUDING THOUGHTS

Children spend many hours each day for several years in child care. The quality of that care is important to their emotional, social, and cognitive development. The quality of care is not merely luck; research shows that there are certain characteristics that predict positive outcomes for children. Child care centers and child care homes that are both licensed and accredited have more of the characteristics that predict positive outcomes. We as parents should ask many questions about the caregiver, the facility, and the activities before choosing child care.

77% of perpetrators of child maltreatment are parents; an additional 11% are other relatives of the victim.

Source: U.S. Department of Health and Human Services. *Child Maltreatment 1996: Reports from the States to the National Child Abuse and Neglect Data System,* Washington, D.C.: U.S. Government Printing Office, 1998.

TALES OF THREE INCEST SURVIVORS

This chapter presents the histories of three child abuse survivors. As you read these stories, we hope you will see the consequences parents' actions can have on their children. Research has shown that the most important influence in a child's life is through his or her parents.

JON'S STORY
Jon Boyer

About 9 years ago I was sitting in a classroom, listening to a police chief instructing the class on the use of firearms. I remember his words explicitly: "Guns are made for one purpose and one purpose only, and that is to kill." I also remember my inability at the time to fathom the circumstances that might cause me to take another's life. As I continued my studies in the administration of justice, those circumstances began to manifest themselves.

An incident occurred involving the beating death of an infant. I tried to imagine my reaction as a police officer responding to the call for this particular disturbance. It was then that I dropped out of college for the second time. It was then that I realized I had allowed my feelings to go unchecked for far too long. It was then that I welcomed in the new year by saying, "This new year will either make me or break me."

Four months later my prophecy proved itself, although I'm not quite sure which outcome I experienced. I'm no longer the confused little boy who dreaded Daddy coming into his bedroom to satisfy his perverse sexual pleasures, the frightened little boy fearful of leaving home. I'm merely the confused and frightened, not so young man who is confined to a state prison.

For too many years that little boy struggled through life, getting by one day at a time, dragging heart and soul behind because they were simply too heavy to carry. Yet he managed. For 22 years I managed. I managed to not keep a job for more than a year. I managed to drop out of college not once but twice. I managed to alienate more than a few people from my life. But perhaps my greatest claim to management lies in the guilt and the grief that I have bestowed on my Mom, for surely she can rely on those things much longer than any profit-sharing or Social Security. How did I pull off this extraordinary feat of management you ask? I simply never told her that my Dad ever touched me in any way beyond that of a father and a son.

Some believe that she should have known of the abuse without my having to tell her. Some have asked, "How could she not have known when it was happening so very close?" Perhaps it was her closeness to the situation that blinded her, something like not fully appreciating a Manet painting unless you view it from a slight distance. She knew I was deeply troubled about something and she saw the pain in my heart. I suppose a young boy spending time alone in his room and smashing recently-built models of cars and planes is quite different from a baby boy in diapers crawling the length of the banquet table at his mother's club meeting. Yet I believe with whole-hearted certainty that she was ignorant of the intimacies between her husband and her son. Despite her best efforts to learn the source of my turmoil, I maintained the distance from her. I kept "my Daddy's secret." I resolved to reveal absolutely nothing, realizing years later the tremendous cost of maintaining that silence and resolve both to myself and to those around me.

Could all of this have been prevented? Perhaps. Could my Mom have been educated in a way to help her recognize child abuse? Maybe. She certainly knows more about it now than when it was occurring. Unfortunately, this state of higher learning has left her nearly crippled with guilt, weeping away the days spent without a son whom she rescued from the brink of death, whom she nurtured and loved.

I have tried to lighten her burden of guilt. I have tried to explain that she had no way of knowing. Yet she refuses to accept this and considers it to be the failing of a mother. I'm sure she has asked herself a great many times, "How could I have recognized what was going on without his telling me?" This is a difficult question to answer. However, let me reflect on some of the things I believe to be indicators of the relationship my Dad and I had.

Perhaps the strongest indicators were the attention I gave to my father and, equally strong, the lack of attention I received from him. Granted, my father gave me quite a bit of his lustful, abusive attention, yet even that attention came to a halt when I was 10 years old. Although we–my father, my mother, my brother, and I–ate supper together, appeared in church together, and took the occasional vacation together, my father and I rarely spent time as father and son. Admittedly, there were infrequent Wiffleball games and fishing trips, yet when I would present a finished model of a car or airplane to him, the local, national, and world news came first, with the all-too-frequent words of, "Not now." When I would present a well-above-average report card to him, he would simply sign it without comment. It was only a matter of time before the models found their way into the trash, smashed and broken into more pieces than they had come in. Soon after, my interest in the report cards followed, with my grades dropping to below average. It was not as if I could not do the work to achieve straight As; I simply would not do the work. Without realizing it at the time, I warranted much more attention with Cs and Ds than with As and Bs.

When it came to simple tasks, such as sawing tree limbs, raking mulch, or painting bicycle frames, my father demanded that things be done in a certain manner, according to a specific order that I could never begin to understand even though I was often told—a manner and an order that did not allow for shortcuts, variations, or independent thinking. Yet I did think independently.

I thought I needed a father—maybe not just a father, but a dad. At least I've learned to appreciate the difference. I also thought that I could somehow persuade my own father to be a dad, or at least someone I felt was one.

However, the lack of attention I received from my father was certainly made up for by my Mom. She was fully aware that some inner turmoil was brewing in me. She constantly asked, "Son, what's wrong?" "Nothing. I'm fine," became my unfailing response. I guess it's not an easy thing to watch the child to whom you gave birth grow up in evident pain, to watch the bright, innocent, inquisitive eyes cloud over in despair. Yet she was forced to stand by and watch because I allowed her to do nothing else. I had focused my attention on my father, thereby neglecting the attention my mother offered me.

I deeply regret the trials she endured—how often she must have felt unwanted and unloved by her son, how often she must have laid awake at night weeping through her prayers for me, how easy it could have been for some people to abandon the hope and the love they profess for others. Yet my mother held fast to her hope and her love for me, as if her life, or perhaps my life, depended on it. Her belief that she failed me because she didn't know what was happening between my father and me is a point for debate. However, undebatable is her greatest testament to motherhood. She stood by me when I was caught shoplifting and stealing. She stood by me after

I killed a man. She stood by me through all of this, naive and vulnerable, without any knowledge of the cause of my turmoil. She stood by me with unfailing, unconditional love, a beautiful and wondrous gift.

I've learned a great deal about love in the last few years, and I would like to say that I loved my father. However, I believe it is more accurate to say that I wanted to love him. Yet in life, he would simply not allow it.

The signs were there, of course.

- The lack of attention shown me by my father, except during perceived threats that his reputation would be sullied.

- The near-hero worship of him on my part.

- The aggression I exhibited toward my models and the walls of my room.

- The extreme introversion I exhibited as a young child, a teenager, and an adult.

- The solitude in which I enveloped myself.

- The lack of interest I had in any of the typical activities of a child my age.

- The stealing and drug usage in an attempt to gain my father's attention.

- The complete lack of surprise and emotion when my father left home.

As I look back on all that has happened, I did reveal "my Daddy's secret" through my behavior. However, to untrained eyes and ears, I revealed only that I was experiencing problems, most of which may be considered part of normal adolescent behavior. Yet there is absolutely nothing normal about children being used for an adult's personal pleasure, nothing normal about children being denied the right to be children, and nothing normal about destroying the innocent spirit of a precious child. According to ancient Celtic legend, the race of faeries, who were infertile, incapable of reproducing at will, protected their children with vehemence. Perhaps if humans were less fertile, they would not be so abusive to their own.

THE RAMIFICATIONS OF CHILD SEXUAL ABUSE
Stacey Ann Lannert

Picture in your mind an 8-year-old girl. She has blonde hair and blue eyes—not beautiful, just average. She has a pretty smile. She is missing a few teeth, but she is proud of those missing teeth. She dreams of being a gymnast, of competing in the Olympics. The only pain she has experienced is a skinned knee and being told, "No."

Now, picture the same little 8-year-old girl lying in a small pool of her own blood. She cannot move, she cannot scream—she is incapacitated. She has just been forced to the ground by the one man she loved, trusted, and respected the most. As he forces her jeans off her, she learns fear. When he penetrates her, a searing pain shatters her soul and numbs her mind. The 8-year-old girl who loved to laugh and play has just become entombed, and her childhood, her innocence have become her burial shroud.

The little 8-year-old girl was me, Stacey Ann Lannert. However, she could have been anyone—a child you see in the store, your neighbor's child, your niece, or your own daughter. The man was my father, yet he too could have been anyone—a schoolteacher, a neighbor, an uncle, or a babysitter. Molested children and child molesters do not wear signs. It would be a much better world if they did. You cannot help someone unless you know that person needs help. Usually, a sexually abused child will not voluntarily come forward and admit that he or she is being abused.

People always tell me, "You should have told someone." Only people who are not abused think it is easy. It's not! There are so many aspects that surround a sexually abused child. I refer to people who have not been abused as "normal people." Normal people cannot understand the weakness, the threats, the torture, and, underneath of it all, the love that come into play. Normal people do not expect to see love in the same category as threats, torture, and weakness, yet in my case it was there.

Even though Dad hurt me, I still loved him. He was a constant in my short life. He was at one point in time my champion, my hero. My young mind made excuses for his behavior. I separated him into two people. This man who hurt me was not my Daddy. I did not know this man; this man was Tom. He was mean, had evil eyes, and his breath always reeked of alcohol. Tom hurt me. On the other hand, Daddy loved me; he hugged me, protected me, and tickled me. Tom scared me, hurt me, and raped me. By separating his personalities, I was able to love and adore him on one level, yet fear and hate him on another level. It was the only way I could survive.

The mind is amazing when it comes to protecting us, although while it protects it also harms. My mind learned early how to disassociate, how to distance myself from the abuse. Disassociation allowed me to not be "in" when he raped me. My mind would go somewhere else and take me with it. I could float away while he was violating my body. I could clean up afterward without even knowing I was cleaning up. My mind had a co-pilot switch that it flipped on when it needed help. To me, that is disassociation—the co-pilot.

While disassociation was helpful, it was also harmful. I have many repressed memories I cannot recall at will that come back to haunt me. Little ghosts haunting the recesses of my mind—they are the memories called flashbacks. Flashbacks never leave, but are always there, waiting. Waiting for a sound or a smell to trigger them. Even now, they are as devastating as the actual event. I am 24 years old, yet I can instantly be transformed into an 8-year-old, a 14-year-old, or any age when he hurt me. Flashbacks are always lurking.

I went through many stages as a result of the abuse. For a period of time, I tried to be perfect. I rationalized that if I were perfect, he wouldn't want to hurt me or to punish me. When it didn't work, I did the opposite. I thought I must be bad inside somewhere I couldn't see. I had to be bad inside or else he wouldn't be hurting me and punishing me. I hurt the people who loved me the most. I took little things from them. I lied to them about petty things. Then I started shoplifting. I would always get caught. Then people would ask, "Why?" I always replied, "I don't know." Yet the whole time my mind would scream, "Because I'm bad! I'm a bad girl! You don't care!"

I did not trust other people. They could hurt me, too, or they might find out what was going on. Dad brainwashed me against Mom. He took words and events out of context and turned me against her. He made me believe that she knew about the abuse but that she didn't care. I never had best friends, at least not for very long. I had boyfriends, but even they were kept at an arm's length. I became superficial. No one knew the real me—no one would love the real me. They only saw the outside, and they only loved the outside. I constantly changed friends, I hurt boyfriends—all to keep them from getting too close. I would not let people get close to me because I thought once they knew what was inside of me, they would run away in disgust. I felt different from everyone else. I would see them and try to mimic them, but inside I knew I was different. I was a fraud; I only pretended to be like them. I was pretty outside, but ugly inside—ugly and dead. I could be surrounded by people, yet I was utterly alone.

Escape was futile. If I told him to stop or I would tell, he threatened me or he laughed at me. If he thought I was becoming too independent, he would punish me. In an even more demeaning manner, he would humiliate me. He would drag me back down to where he kept me subservient to only him. I became weaker and he became more controlling. He took away everyone I ever loved until there was only him. I became conditioned like one of Pavlov's dogs—I stopped looking for a way to escape. Escape to where? He always brought me back to him, always destroyed me, always.

Somewhere during the abuse I lost my will to live. Waking to another day meant waking to another day of pain. I became a changeling—one child substituted for another. I became accepting, depressed, and hollow. I learned weakness—remoteness—fear. I lost the knowledge of everything I knew. I lost God. I lost my mother. I lost myself.

The sexual abuse I endured changed every square inch of my world. My eyes now see the world from a perspective that is different from that of normal people. I am not normal but different. I suffered vicious, violent rapes at the hands of my father. The same man who was supposed to teach me love, respect, morals, and values instead taught me pain, humiliation, torture, and fear. My father–my perpetrator, my tormentor–taught me the true coldness of the world in one unprovoked attack. My life as a child ended because of that attack, and my reality became distorted as a result.

I will never be normal, but I will heal. I will never forget, but I will forgive. My life will continue, and I will continue to grow emotionally. Now that it is over, I no longer live day in and day out with fear. Now that the truth is out, I no longer hide the real me. Now I have found the real me.

Normal people do not understand how abuse affects a child. They cannot understand the never-ending nightmare, the distorted reality, the learned behavior, the constant inner turmoil, or the pain. Many normal people have said to me, "It's over—just get over it!" Unfortunately, it's not that simple. Sexual abuse is not something a person just "gets over." People have more sympathy for a woman raped on the street once by a stranger than they do for a child raped repeatedly in her own bed by someone she loves. I am not trying to downplay the tragedy of a rape victim—rape is rape. However, explain to a child why Daddy hurts her over and over again. Children cannot comprehend, nor can they–nor should they–be expected to understand.

Maybe the best way to explain how I feel the abuse affected my life is to compare myself to an inanimate object. Before the abuse I was a pretty porcelain doll. The first time I was raped, the porcelain doll was shattered into pieces. I put myself back together, but the pieces would not fit together correctly. Each time I was raped the pieces would be smashed again, thus becoming more mixed up and more difficult to put back together. Eventually the pieces were smashed so much that all that was left was a fine porcelain powder. There was nothing left to put back together—no longer a way to fix me. Everything about me, everything that was me, slowly disappeared. Yet unlike the porcelain doll, what was left were the emotions—the fear, the pain, and the hopelessness.

Seeing the face of a child makes me question the human race today. When I see the innocence of a bright-eyed child, I wonder why certain people can bring such hell into a child's life. Sexual abuse, incest, and molestation create a hell that changes a child—and these changes affect the child's dreams, the child's emotions, and the child's outcome in life.

I am no longer a victim—I am now a survivor. It is not easy, nor will it ever become easy. I still remember and I still struggle to forgive. I yearn to forget, but forgetting would be losing a part of myself. I must cope, adapt, and overcome, but I will never forget. I must have faith in God. I must have faith in those I love. I must have faith in myself.

I have faith in the parents of today and the children of tomorrow. We must as a nation, as a people, come together and stop child abuse. I implore you to take the time to learn the signs of an abused child, to take the time to look for the signs in a child, and to take the time to help a child when you see the signs. Ask yourself one question: Would you deliberately walk past a child in need of help? Each time you ignore a child's cry for help, you are deliberately walking past a child. . . maybe even your own child.

AN INCEST STORY
M. Susan Clements

My name is Sue. I am 47 years old and I am a survivor of childhood incest. Today, the term *survivor* rather than *victim* more accurately describes me. This is the result of hard work in therapy and support groups, as well as having wonderful, nurturing friends who helped me every step of the way.

What I want to focus on is that, although I am an incest survivor, I don't have to live the hopeless and desperate existence that I once felt doomed to live. I can (and did) get help, and I found it was possible to heal from the trauma of incest and live a reasonably happy life. To accomplish this, I need to tell you what it was like for me during the incest experience, what I did to heal from it, and what life is like for me today. Be certain that I am not, by any stretch of the imagination, completely healed—this, I have come to learn, is a lifelong process. I am, however, on the upward swing of that process. Here is my story.

I know little about my mother's family history and even less about my biological father's family history. What I do know is that my biological father was an alcoholic and an only child who died at the age of 42 of alcoholism. His mother (my grandmother) never married. My mother was born and raised in Vienna, Austria and has one brother and one sister. When my mother left Austria to come to America (she married my father when he was a GI in the Army), her mother and her brother moved to Brazil. My grandmother had another child (my mother's younger sister) after she emigrated to Brazil. My mother's biological father died in World War I, and I know nothing of him or of any of my mother's stepfathers (my grandmother outlived at least four husbands). Mother was 16 years old when she left Austria and did not see her mother again for 37 years, when she came to the United States for a visit. My mother left my father and ran off with one of his friends when I was about 4 years old. She left my father because he drank and became violent when he was drunk. After she ran off with my father's friend, I never saw my father again. It is the man my mother ran off with (I'll call him "the perpetrator") who molested me from the age of about 5 until I left home at 19. He also molested most of my other siblings, although most of them choose to remain in denial. The perpetrator is now 74 years old and in poor health. My mother is still with him.

The family I grew up in was very dysfunctional and chaotic. I was the second to the oldest in a blended family of 10 children. There were five boys and five girls. Mother brought three, the perpetrator brought two, and they made five more. There is 15 years' difference between me and the last child. The house I grew up in was a very small three-bedroom frame house that didn't have a basement and had only one bathroom. Privacy was never honored, whether you were changing clothes or taking a bath. Sleeping arrangements were at a premium. There were five girls in one bedroom, five boys in the second bedroom, and my mother and the perpetrator in the third bedroom. Two sets of bunk beds were in each of our bedrooms, so most of us at least had our own bed. My bunk was on top. When a room addition was built onto the house, it was given to their first-born son. He did not have to share his new bedroom with any of the other brothers, even though there were two brothers who were older than he. This son is also a perpetrator of sexual abuse (but not mine).

I have always remembered the incest. My memories go back to when it started—I was about 5 years old. One of my first memories is the perpetrator's brother climbing into bed with me one afternoon while I was trying to take a nap and reaching up under my dress, tugging at my panties. I remember trying to yell, but I was hushed up. It's not clear in my memory whether I told my mother about it or not. I was always very scared.

Another experience that occurred when I was about 11 years old is also very vivid in my memory. As a child, I was always smaller than the other children and very underdeveloped, but not really fragile. I remember my mother working the second shift at the factory and it being a summer evening, just before dark. I had been playing outside with my brothers and sisters when the perpetrator called me inside. He was lying on his bed and called me to his side. There is a blank between that moment and the moment he began trying to penetrate my small vagina with his huge penis.

I am so very, very frightened and crying for him to stop. He is making lewd sexual slurs that arouse him. As he looks down on me crying out for him to stop, I have no features that resemble a grown woman—not even pubic hair—I am only a little girl. He cannot penetrate my small opening. When he finishes (without penetration), he puts fifty or seventy-five cents in my hand and sends me back outside to play. Because I take the money, I am as guilty as he is.

It was an unspoken rule that I would not say a word about what happened to anybody. This is not something I could share even with my sisters. You see, I know he was doing it to them and to the boys, too, because I would lie awake at night and be relieved when he chose someone else. We never talked about it among ourselves—ever. But we all knew it was happening.

Another incident that is particularly clear occurred when I was 13 years old and homebound from school because of some complicated back surgery that left me helpless to move around. I was confined in a body cast that weighed more than I did at that time (I weighed 85 pounds and the cast weighed 95 pounds!). The perpetrator took advantage of my extreme vulnerability during this time to satisfy his own sick needs. As a patrolman for the local police department, he could come home whenever he wanted. One day while my mother was working days and my brothers and sisters were in school, he showed up for one of his impromptu visits. This visit was not just to check up on me. The perpetrator had other plans.

He comes into the bedroom where I am confined because I am unable to move around much. He proceeds to pull his trousers down around his ankles and he pulls out his penis and shoves it inside my mouth to suck. I am helpless to move, fight, or get away from the perpetrator because part of the body cast goes up behind my head and he is able to hold that part (and me) steadfast. The perpetrator does not stop until he finishes in my mouth. He tries to force me to swallow, but I gag and hobble to the bathroom to spit it out. Once again, he shoves money into my hand. Once again, the guilt shifts from him to me. Then he gets into his patrol car and returns to work as if nothing has happened.

Some time later, I did tell my mother. Her response was, "I'll talk to him about it." When I went back to her later, she said, "He denied it." Nothing more was ever mentioned. Devastated by my mother's response and her lack of action or protection, I never again confided in my mother, although the molesting continued until I left home at age 19. Since mothers were supposed to protect and love, I believed in my heart that I was responsible for what was happening. I felt like a whore who took money for a dirty deed—and my mother validated how I felt when she took the perpetrator's side. I was all alone. I felt doomed to live a life of despair. I felt like a horrible person because I did these dirty deeds and I knew God had been watching me commit these sinful acts. Even the thought of suicide did not offer the relief I was seeking because I knew I'd go to hell if I killed myself—and since I was already in hell, why bother? Existing as a mere shell of a non-person was the best I could hope for.

Leaving home did not rid me of the feelings of despair and worthlessness, and I barely existed. Over and over I found myself in situations where I would be sexually molested by men. Only then, because I was a consenting adult, I did not view it as "molestation." Then I saw it as a willing act on my part even if I did not want to have sex. I felt unable to say no or to stand up for myself. When I was a child and told the perpetrator to stop, he never listened. Why would it be different when I told other men to stop? They would never listen either. So I became a victim of my own making. Others saw me as very willing and hot-to-trot for sex. But on the inside, I was actually dying or already dead. I was repeating what my perpetrator had done for years and I didn't know how to stop it.

Over the next 20+ years, I drifted from one abusive relationship to another, never knowing why but always believing I didn't deserve better. Abuses ranged from sexual to physical to emotional to all three. My physical health began to suffer as a result of stress and my inability to accept life on life's terms, and I felt hopeless and doomed. It never occurred to me that my incest experiences as a child were affecting every facet of my life as an adult. In fact, it was seeking help for the effects of my grown children's alcoholism that led me to get help for myself. What I learned changed my life. I learned that the devastating effects of incest have been compared to the suffering of prisoners of war in a concentration camp. Every fiber of human dignity is stripped away. The effects linger as the years go by, and if help is not sought, being a "victim" and continuing to choose people who are "perpetrators" of one sort or another will follow like an ominous cloud. This is because we don't know how not to be a victim or how to choose healthy people who won't harm us. As victims, we are easy prey for all sorts of undesirables.

Today, I am no longer a victim and I can once again view the world as a beautiful place. I am confident and self-assured. I am the most important person in my life and I am worthwhile. I believe in a Power greater than myself (who I call God) and I know He would never hurt me. God gave man the gift of free will and will not rescind that gift or interfere unless He is asked to do so. It was my perpetrator's free will and choice to molest me as a child. To endure such pain, God also gave me the gift of shutting down emotionally. This was how I survived most of my life. Today, God wants me to be happy, joyous, and free—and, for the most part, today I am. Although confronting the family with the incest secret has labeled me as a troublemaker and a black sheep by those who choose to remain in denial, for me it has meant freedom and release far greater than anything I could have imagined. I encourage you to get help if you are a victim of incest. Telling the secret out loud to those who care can be the difference between being alive and being among the walking dead.

Research shows that abuse victims are six times more likely to abuse their own children or others.

Source: (website) Georgia Council on Child Abuse, Inc. *The Statistics*, http://www.gcca.org/stat/index.html

PARENTS WHOSE CHILDREN WERE ABUSED

JOAN BOYER AND DEB UNDERWOOD

Deb and I have become each other's support system. We share a common bond through our painful experiences with our children. We have discovered that their behaviors were extremely similar.

We have also learned through our conversations with one another that there were definite personality similarities between our late husbands.

- *Both were very controlling individuals.*

- *Neither of them wanted their wife to work or have any knowledge or control over the finances. Both of us concluded that we felt like possessions of our husbands and certainly not equal partners in any aspect of the relationship.*

- *We both feel that they stressed the importance of impressions made on outsiders. In both instances, people who knew both our families felt that we were the "perfect family"; image was everything.*

- *The emphasis in both our families was the husband—what he wanted and what made him happy was the primary focus of the marriage. The husband's needs came first, and he had the final word in all that took place.*

- *Both of our husbands were extremely ambitious for success, seeming to be driven toward that end.*

- *Both had competitive and unloving relationships with their own fathers. Both seemed to accelerate in strange behaviors after the deaths of their fathers.*

- *Both were loners. Neither had any close friends.*

- *Both were secretive and manipulative.*

- *Both were extremely critical and judgmental.*

- *Both gave the impression to other people of being arrogant and superior.*

- *Both were typical workaholics.*

- *Both had mothers who appeared to feel their sons could do no wrong and doted on them.*

- *Both were extremely particular about their possessions, e.g., tools, and would become angry if anyone, especially the children, used them and did not replace them in the exact same spot and position. Everything had to be in an exact order.*

- *Both seemed to enjoy inflicting the cruelest type of emotional pain.*

- *Family vacations, or outings, which were few, were what they wanted. No consideration was given to what other family members wanted. Both shied away from family functions unless it was with their side of the family.*

WARNING SIGNS EVERY PARENT SHOULD KNOW
Joan Boyer

My name is Joan. I am the mother of two sons, one of whom I know with certainty is the victim of childhood sexual abuse. I strongly suspect that the other son was likewise abused, but this has not been confirmed. My older son was born during my first marriage which lasted 5 years. He was not yet 2 years old when we divorced. I remarried and my second son was born. That marriage ended in divorce 21 years later. After the birth of my second son, I began to suspect that my husband was homosexual; however, there was no confirmation of this fact until after the divorce. Six years later, I learned that my ex-husband was not only a homosexual, but that he was also a pedophile who had sexually abused our younger son, Jon.

The events that led to the discovery of the abuse were tragic in themselves. The need to prove that abuse had occurred so many years earlier took on a life of its own. It truly became a struggle for life or death where my son was concerned, and therefore for me. Jon had shot and killed his father.

When I look back on those 21 years of marriage, there is much sadness, anger, and frustration related to the knowledge that my son was sexually abused. There is also a self-imposed guilt that doesn't want to go away. Throughout my son's life I knew there was something wrong with the picture, so to speak, but my background and knowledge and the very times themselves did not provide me with any concrete answers as to what that "something wrong" might be. Never in my wildest dreams would I have imagined incest was taking place within the confines of our home.

I came from a hard-working, middle-class Catholic family. I had a very protective, nurturing mother and a father who thoroughly enjoyed spending time with his children. My parents loved and sacrificed for each other and for their family. I was especially close to my Dad. Until the day he died, I knew that he always put my welfare ahead of his own. He was my best friend, my Dad. He was what I thought all dads were. In looking back, I realize that the relationship I had with my Dad influenced my thinking with respect to my children and their father. My childhood was not perfect, but in the traditional sense of normal, it came very close. However, my relatively sheltered childhood did not prepare me for what I was to experience in my own marriage. Furthermore, my preconceived notions of what fathers were or should be would ultimately cloud my reality.

There were so many strange and extenuating circumstances that entered into Jon's life that it distorted my reasoning, making it difficult to distinguish what was at the core of his problem. Jon required surgery at the age of 5 weeks to correct what was diagnosed as a feeding problem causing malnutrition. He recovered well, but I was told that there could be subsequent mental or physical impairment, and only time would tell. Jon later developed bone age retardation, possibly as a result of the malnutrition, and was treated with hormones when he was 9 years old. A few years later, a tumor was discovered in his leg, being a side effect of the treatment for the bone age retardation, and subsequent surgery at age 15 was needed. These were only some of the physical issues that contributed to my confusion.

During the feeding problem episode, I encountered an attitude from Jon's father that was disturbing to me, but one that would prevail throughout our marriage. When I voiced my concern about Jon's condition, Terry insisted that my imagination was working overtime. He continued by saying he "could not produce a defective child." I could not believe the words I was hearing. When I mentioned that I was operating on "gut level feelings," as I called them, I was ridiculed for not being logical. My own confusion kicked in and this was the beginning of many years of intellectualizing and rationalizing behaviors that defied reason.

The first few years of Jon's life, I was gifted with a bright, extroverted, curiously adventurous happy child. His big dark eyes would light up and dance in recognition of each new wonder to which he was exposed. Suddenly, and without any obvious explanation, a transformation occurred. His eyes, which now appeared to be lifeless and fixed, gave me the first indication that something was wrong with my child. I also could not understand the timid, withdrawn, easily frightened preschooler who emerged. Again, Jon's father insisted that I was imagining things, and the doctors who examined Jon could find no basis for my concern.

It was when Jon was between the ages of 3 and 4 that I recall sleeping problems began to occur, along with occasional bed wetting. In and of themselves, these problems did not seem to be out of the ordinary for a child Jon's age. However, it reached a point where Jon did not want to sleep in his room because of the "monsters." Jon either could not or would not articulate to me what these "monsters" were.

Jon began to resist being put to bed in the evenings. He also began to experience frightening nightmares and would wake up screaming. My thought was that perhaps Jon's older brother, or his friends, had frightened him with the idea of monsters. Many nights, I would lie down with Jon and eventually fall asleep in his bed. This upset Terry, who accused me of trying to make a "sissy" out of Jon.

A part of Jon's bedtime routine was to kneel at the side of his bed with me and say our nighttime prayers. This was a beautiful memory for me for many years—until I learned of the abuse. I remember Jon praying "God bless Mommy and Daddy and Randy and me and make me a good boy. Help me to always mind Mommy and Daddy." A prayer to his Guardian Angel would follow. I never thought to tell him that he should not "mind" Mommy or Daddy if they ever touched him in a place that was not comfortable for him. I also never thought to explain to him that he and Daddy (or anyone else for that matter) should not have secrets from Mommy. I recall those moments now and instead of joy I feel tremendous guilt. The guilt is there because Jon recently shared with me that during his childhood there were times when he thought that I must know what his father was doing to him. The prayers to always "mind" Daddy were coming from me. The Guardian Angel that I assured Jon would always protect him didn't seem to be doing a very good job as seen through the eyes of a little boy who was being sexually abused.

The sleep problems became sporadic but they did continue. Jon was now coming into our bedroom and lying on the floor at the foot of our bed. He would be discovered and moved into his room. Later he would lie on the floor on my side of the bed. Many times I would awaken and almost step on him. (I have learned that Jon reasoned that if he laid on my side of the bed, his father didn't bother him.)

An incident at the K-Mart store when Jon was about 6 years old was also troubling to me, but not to Terry. Jon had picked up two Matchbox cars and hid them in his sock. A security guard saw it and we were stopped at the door. At first Jon lied about the cars but it was obvious that they were protruding in his sock. The guard retrieved the cars, said a few frightening things to Jon, and we left the store. A similar incident occurred several years later at Six Flags with the same results. I was beginning to think I was completely crazy. I could not accept that these were normal childhood behaviors. Was I that abnormal? I didn't do these things when I was a child.

I recall having to buy new underwear for Jon more often than I thought should have been necessary. I began to think that he was having accidents and didn't want anyone to know so he would just throw the underwear away. We were also experiencing problems with the sewer lines backing up, but I must confess I never made the connection. I have since learned that Jon would flush his underwear down the toilet both at home and at school because it was bloody.

There were many hints throughout the years when Jon was growing up that something was wrong. The "something" is what continued to remain the mystery. **I realize now that if you are not familiar with or expecting to find sexual abuse, it will escape you.** When I would clean Jon's room, I would find clean pieces of paper crumbled and discarded in the wastepaper basket. My gut level feeling was that Jon wanted to put something down on paper but couldn't and in frustration would crumple the paper and throw it away, again and again. There were also National Football League pencils—something he treasured and never sharpened—that I found broken in two and discarded. Likewise with some of his favorite toys. I could almost feel Jon's anger when I found these things. When mentioning this to Terry, I was made to feel guilty for not allowing Jon "his space" as he put it. Even doctors with whom I spoke never once suggested the possibility of abuse.

Jon spent a great deal of time alone in his room. He resisted going outside and playing. I recall coming home one afternoon when Terry was watching the boys and finding Jon sitting in the closet in his room. I was shocked. It was a beautiful sunny day and my little boy was sitting in a dark closet with the door closed. Why? His simple answer was that he wanted to read with a flashlight. His father didn't see anything wrong with this. According to Terry, Jon was not as extroverted as I and had different interests. Jon was more like his side of the family. I was told to accept the differences and stop thinking there was something wrong with him. Perhaps Jon was just like Terry. I knew that Jon idolized his father and, at times, I felt that I had no importance to Jon, and that hurt.

Jon was about 10 years old when an incident occurred that frightened me tremendously. His father and I had attended an evening open house at school, leaving Randy, who was now 15, to sit with Jon for a few hours. When we came home, I saw the word "S H I T" written in lipstick on the wall. It seemed like such an angry message. I knew in my heart that Jon had written it. To this day, I can recall the fear and the pain for my child that seemed to engulf me. The lipstick made me think it had something to do with me and that certainly got my attention. Terry made no comment about it and didn't seem to register any emotion. This was not too unusual, however, because Terry seldom registered any show of emotion. I was the one who asked the boys if they could explain how the word got on the wall.

Randy seemed surprised when he saw it and denied any knowledge. Jon, too, denied having written it. I recall sitting on the edge of Jon's bed and telling him I sensed he was angry about something. I told him that it was all right to be angry but that he needed to tell someone why he felt that way so that we could have an opportunity to fix whatever was wrong. He insisted that he was not angry, there was nothing wrong, and he had not written on the wall. **This incident was especially disturbing to me because I realized that my child was lying to me when there was no apparent reason to lie.** This was to become my first real encounter with years of senseless, habitual lying from Jon.

I immediately had a discussion with Terry and suggested that we take Jon to a psychologist. I felt very strongly that something was definitely wrong with Jon. As in the past, Terry minimized my concerns and insisted that I was over-reacting to what is typical child behavior. I might mention here that Terry minored in child psychology at college and I had no formal training in that area. After months of my insistence, Terry finally conceded to setting up an appointment with a child psychologist. The three of us had our scheduled session with Terry laying the groundwork. I was allowed to voice my concerns. Jon was called in and spoke only briefly. It was concluded by the psychologist that Terry needed to spend more time with Jon. Terry took Jon fishing for 2 hours and that was to be the solution to Jon's problems.

It was either shortly before or shortly after the wall art incident that I began to notice a serious distancing between Terry and Jon. Prior to that time, Terry would interrupt conversations with anyone in our extended family when Jon came into the group, making certain that Jon recognized Terry was there. The situation changed dramatically. **Terry now seemed to avoid Jon completely. He showed no interest in anything that pertained to Jon. When interaction between them did occur, Jon met with sarcasm or criticism.** I attempted to bring this to Terry's attention many times because it was clearly affecting Jon, but I never got a response—Terry would simply appear to listen to what I had to say and stare off into space. In retrospect, I realize I did get a response. Terry's response was to pursue another degree or begin another project. In that way he could legitimately avoid my questions or comments.

The 1960s and 1970s were to me a difficult time to raise children because attitudes were changing so rapidly. The sexual revolution brought with it many confusions to someone who was raised in a strait-laced, parochial atmosphere, but who also was open to keeping up with the times. I found this to be especially true in dealing with the pornographic materials of Terry's that I would find stashed in the utility room or workshop. **As long as the boys didn't have access to the pornography, I tried to accept its presence without saying**

anything to Terry about it. However, it became embarrassing to me when I took his suits to the cleaners and, upon checking the pockets, the clerk found pictures, pages from books, and other paraphernalia. From that time on, I simply asked Terry to take whatever was in his pockets out before he asked me to drop off anything at the cleaners. To this day, I still have the feeling that Terry wanted me to find these things and he wanted to get some type of response from me. I realize now how serious the mind-games and the manipulation were. Strangely enough, in the midst of them, that awareness doesn't have the same impact.

The silence regarding the pornography issue reached its limit when I learned that Jon, who was now about 15, was concealing magazines that could only be described as perverse. No "innocent" Playboy stuff. This was hard core porn. I'm not sure why I bothered to bring this to Terry's attention, but I did. At that point, however, I didn't care that Terry felt this was normal for a young man Jon's age. I also didn't care that Terry felt I had invaded Jon's privacy. **My concern was that my young son should not get some distorted ideas about sex before he ever had an opportunity to experience healthy and beautiful sharing with a female. Little did I know.** I told Terry that if he would not back me, I would confront Jon myself. Terry refused to get involved. I don't know if I handled the situation properly, but I did the best I could. I confessed to Jon that I had found the books and that I wanted to know why he felt it necessary to hide them. Jon said he didn't know, which was a standard answer for most questions. Being ever aware of not "warping his psyche," as Terry would say, I offered a suggestion to Jon for determining the criteria for reading materials. I asked him if he felt comfortable with me putting the magazines on the living room table for others to enjoy. He immediately said, "No." I tried to explain to him that this is not what healthy, loving relationships were about. I then threw the magazines in the trash.

Three years later, Terry and I were divorced; Jon was 18. I was relieved. During our tenth year of marriage I had told Terry that I wanted a divorce. There had been no intimacy and little or no physical contact between Terry and I since Jon's birth. I felt I could no longer function in what I described as a "time bomb" atmosphere: always knowing that episodes of emotional abuse were imminent but never knowing when they would strike. Jon apparently overheard our conversation one night and told my mother that he would kill himself if we got a divorce. It would be all his fault. Knowing how much Jon loved his father, I reconsidered. I now know Jon's pain went much deeper than I could have ever realized at the time.

It is tragic to know that Jon "existed" as best he could in his distorted childhood, that he must have struggled daily with the requirements of maturity in his teen years, and that because of the lack of maturity, he was erroneously accused of being lazy and having no sense of direction in his life. It is not difficult to realize that his feelings of inadequacy and his lack of self-esteem were constantly reinforced. He was emotionally and psychologically crippled with his programmed guilt, shame, confusion, and fear. I did not realize and, tragically, he did not fully realize why he was so "different," and because he could not disclose his secret, the psychologists did not diagnose his problem, and he was not helped. It wasn't until after months of incarceration that he finally shared with me that he had been abused. The puzzle pieces now began to fit. I sought to learn as much as I could about abuse.

Jon's visit to Ohio in 1990 was the first occasion since his father and I divorced in 1984 that he had spent any "alone time" with his father. He was with his father only 5-1/2 days when the tragedy occurred. Jon had never had a history of violence . . . until that day. I have since learned that being isolated with his perpetrator was the worst case scenario for Jon. He tried to confront his father with questions about the abuse and in the process he regressed back to the time when the abuse was occurring. The psychologists call it posttraumatic stress disorder. Jon was also diagnosed as having dissociative disorder.

Jon, like so many other sexually abused children, learned to suppress every emotion and every feeling. To survive, he could not allow himself to feel the emotional pain. Many, like the former Miss America, Marilyn Vandebur Atler, develop what they call their "night child" and their "day child." Each entity acts independently of the other and without the knowledge of the other's existence. Ironically, in the process of suppressing their emotions to ward off the pain, they also prevent themselves from feeling any joy or happiness or genuine love. They have a very difficult time relating to people in a one-to-one relationship and consequently many never experience any form of intimacy.

Knowing that the abuse occurred was one thing, but proving it after so many years was something else. I had saved most of Jon's drawings since he started preschool at age 3. These drawings would eventually become the physical evidence to substantiate the abuse, which, in fact, was already occurring at age 3 (see **Figure 11-1,a to i**). During the trial, a precedent was established in the state of Ohio, which now permits the testimony of art therapists as expert witnesses in the area of childhood sexual abuse (Ohio being the sixteenth state to do so). The court recognized that this was not a premeditated act on Jon's part, and he was therefore found guilty of manslaughter instead of murder.

Where was I while all of Jon's abuse was taking place? I've asked myself that question a thousand times. I was doing all the things that suburban, middle-class American housewives and mothers were supposed to do: mothers' clubs, PTAs, vacation church school, Cub Scouts, room parties, and baking cookies. Should I have thought that my ex-Air Force officer husband who was now a bank vice president, president of our church council, president of our Khoury League, president of the PTA, would not be able to be trusted with his own son? **Child molesters only hung out in public restrooms. They didn't wear a suit and tie and carry a briefcase, and they certainly didn't live in a nice home with a nice family. And above all else, we didn't call them Daddy.** *Wrong!*

I've thought a lot about how easy it is for a perpetrator to manipulate and confuse a child. It wasn't that difficult to manipulate and confuse *me.* Children are such easy prey because they are so trusting and so vulnerable. They want so desperately to please and to be accepted. Jon was told by his father that what they were sharing was a special kind of love between a father and a son. Jon was also told that others would not understand and therefore it had to be their secret. At the age of 3, I feel a child believes all that he or she is told. How confusing it must have been for Jon to experience two distinctly different types of "love" from his father and his mother.

As parents, we have the responsibility to provide many things for our children. It is my feeling that a safe and healthy environment is the most important place to begin. This is not as easy as it may sound, but my feeling is that we must focus on the following:

- Begin by never assuming anything is impossible.

- Educate ourselves as to the red flags of sexual abuse. Being forewarned is being forearmed.

- Pray to God that we will never have to face the problem of childhood sexual abuse, but if we are confronted with it, our primary focus must be getting help for the child.

- Above all, listen to that little inner voice and have the courage and persistence to insist on getting answers.

Unlike when my son was growing up, there are now clinics and agencies that specialize in the diagnosis and treatment of sexual abuse. Use them. Believe me, the problem doesn't go away. It just gets worse.

I would recommend that when your child is old enough to understand, you teach him or her that he or she has the right to say "no" to certain touches. Don't force children to hug or kiss anyone they don't want to. This will only confuse what you are telling them is their right. Let your child know that you always want to know if someone had touched him or her inappropriately. Let your child know that he or she will never be punished for telling you the truth and above all, accept what your child is telling you and assure him or her that you will look into the matter and be there to provide protection. If inappropriate touching has occurred, children must be reassured that it was not their fault and they do not bear any of the guilt.

Don't ever assume that "so and so" would never do anything like that. They just might. It's far better to err on the side of your child. Understand, also, that there are severe long-term ramifications associated with childhood sexual abuse if it goes untreated. The prisons are full of these victims.

Vigilance and diligence are necessary in detecting and combating sexual abuse. Be alert and attentive to the following:

- Any behavioral or personality changes

- Sleep disorders

- Changes in activity levels

- Unexplained fears

- An obvious preference of one parent over the other and a compelling need to have the approval of that parent

- Nervousness

- Isolation

- Reluctance or refusal to shower after gym classes

- Low self-esteem

- Age-inappropriate immaturity

- Uncomfortable feelings with their bodies

- Lying

- Stealing

- Secrecy

- Periods of depression

- Eating disorders

- Preoccupation with sex

- Threats of suicide

- Use of drugs or alcohol

A few of these symptoms may not necessarily indicate sexual abuse, but if a majority of symptoms is present, trust that a pattern has begun to form and, chances are, sexual abuse is taking place.

I am happy to let you know that as bad as the ramifications of abuse are, there is tremendous hope for these courageous survivors. Since disclosing the abuse, my frightened, immature, insecure son has conquered many of his fears and has emerged as a mature, self-confident, intelligent, and articulate young man. Jon has made us all very proud by the way he has conducted himself while being incarcerated. He has had poetry published, he worked daily in Psych Services and now for the Assistant Warden, he has been an exemplary inmate, and his relationship with me is a blessing because he can now verbalize and share his feelings. For the first time in our lives, we can really talk to each other. Jon is compassionate, kind, and sensitive and he has so very much to offer as an advocate of children, hoping to eventually become a spokesperson to help in the fight against abuse. He committed a violent act but he is not a violent person.

This is a poem that Jon wrote that speaks of his feelings as a child going through the agony and trauma of abuse:

Please, Daddy, Don't!

As the bedroom door opens, slowly with a creak,

Under the blanket a child hides, frightened and meek,

Hoping the man standing there would turn and go away,

But knowing why the man has come and that he plans to stay.

The child's screams are lost in the dark of the night,

Strained and choked, silenced with disabling fright

From the impending danger now beginning to loom,

In the darkened corners of the little one's room.

The little one was young in age, without worldly experience,

But nights like these would cripple his growth, and end his innocence.

He had only known hurt and pain from his knees being scraped,

He couldn't understand this pain, this pain of being raped.

The little one created a world where he could feel safe,

A world where, at times like these, he could go and escape,

But always wanting the man to stop, knowing that he won't,

The little one cried and mumbled, "Please, Daddy, don't."

Figure 11-1. This series of drawings was made by Jon throughout his childhood and then as an adult. He killed his father and, in the pretrial period, disclosed that he had been sexually abused by his father beginning at the age of 3 years and ending just before puberty. I had saved his drawings and was able to have an art therapist evaluate them in support of his claim of abuse.

11-1,a. This was drawn while Jon was in preschool. The intensity and choice of colors indicate Jon's emotional state.

11-1,b. Another early drawing. Note the intensity, chaotic quality, and choice of colors.

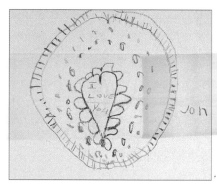

11-1,c.
Here you can see the "encapsulation" theme that was frequently in Jon's drawings—which the art therapist said indicated a desire to set boundaries, to be safe and protected.

11-1,d and **e.** Self-portraits. The therapist pointed out that these are fragmented, primitive, and show him as very small and helpless. Notice that he drew a small sad face isolated in the corner of the page in **e.**

11-1,f. *In this drawing, made while Jon was in art therapy, he describes the abuse. It began with fondling and progressed to anal sex in the bathroom, including enemas. Jon related that he would hide in the closet when I was out of the house and then sneak into our room at night and sleep at the foot of the bed where he felt safe.*

11-1,g *and* **h.** *Jon shows here his feelings about himself and his father and what had happened.*

11-1,i. *Jon depicts his prison life.*

THE SIGNS OF SEXUAL ABUSE AND HOW TO SPOT IT
Deb Underwood

Box 11-1 lists signs of abuse that should trigger your response. They frequently indicate sexual abuse.

Box 11-1. Signs of Sexual Abuse

Little things don't quite seem right.

Child withdraws from you and favors the other parent.

Child has no or low self-esteem.

Child doesn't feel "normal" and states it verbally.

Child has difficulty falling asleep.

Child lies about minor things. Lying becomes a pattern.

Child develops mood swings.

Child develops nervous energy.

Child steals things from others.

Child creates a fantasy world.

Child doesn't own feelings (answers, "I don't know" repeatedly).

Child constantly seeks approval from abusive parent (has approval from other parent).

Child develops outbursts or temper tantrums (occur when least expected).

The best warning sign is your gut instinct that something is wrong. If something doesn't feel right in your gut, then more than likely it isn't right. I had plenty of those gut instinct feelings during the course of raising my two daughters and being married to their father. We were married for 15 years and divorced in 1985. He had a severe drinking problem, although he claimed he didn't. According to him, I was the one with the problem because I couldn't accept his drinking. He started drawing his fists back at me during confrontations and I felt it was only a matter of time before he used his fists back at me, or, God forbid, on the children. Either way, I couldn't let that happen. I grew up in a physically abusive home and that's where I drew the line. That's why I left him—not as much because of the drinking, but because of his uncontrollable temper. He said that I brought out "the beast" in him. He didn't like not getting his way.

One would think that a mother would know if her child were being sexually abused by the other parent. One would also think that it would be easy to spot, especially if the mother had been victimized by her own father as a child. In this case, it had the opposite effect. I trusted my husband and I shouldn't have trusted him. I trusted him as a father because he appeared to be a good father. He didn't believe in spanking. Not once did I see sexual abuse, nor did he ever give me a clue of the abuse. He stated many times that he would kill any "s.o.b." who tried to physically or sexually hurt his daughters. If anything, I grew up in an age where I was naive, even into adulthood. I trusted people until they gave me reason not to trust them.

You need to question little things that don't quite seem right. There were times I heard squeals coming from my daughter when she and her father were downstairs in the family room watching television. This made me feel very uneasy. These squeals sounded the same as the sound I had emitted when I was a child fighting off advances from my father. When I heard the squeals I went downstairs to see what was going on. By the time I got there, my daughter was sitting on the couch and my husband in his easy chair. When I would ask, "Is everything OK?" he said, "Yes, we were just playing." I asked my daughter if that was true and she always agreed with what he said. After what seemed like numerous times of this happening, I'd just call out from the top of the stairs to find out if everything was OK and was told it was. My husband told me that I was making a mountain out of a molehill because I had been molested by my father during my adolescent years. He told me that I was crazy if I thought that he would stoop that low. He told me that I needed psychological help and I thought the worst of him because of my father. He accused me of comparing him to my father and there was no comparison. Then, of course, I questioned myself. Was I over-reacting? Maybe . . . probably . . . . It wasn't fair to compare him with my own deviate father. There was a lot of self-doubt on my part, perhaps because of the abuse, and my husband knew exactly what to say to throw me off the track. I will never forgive myself for not knowing what was going on under my own roof and for not protecting my children from their own father. Every time I questioned him, he always gave a "valid" answer.

Another incident that didn't seem right was when I found bloody underwear under the stairwell in the back of the basement. That was where I sorted the dirty clothes on washday. This area was near the washer and dryer and it was out of view. There was also a toilet, a sink, and a shower in the entrance of that room. One washday morning I found several pairs of bloody underwear under the stairwell. I called both of the girls into the room and questioned them about the underwear. I thought maybe one of them had hurt themselves in the vaginal area. They both denied wearing the underwear and claimed not to know what had happened. Finally, I said I was going to take both of them to the doctor to have them examined because something *had* to be wrong with one of them. At that point, the oldest one admitted that she had started menstruating.

She was too ashamed to come and tell me about it. I thought that it was very strange that she didn't come tell me her "news" and it hurt my feelings to know my daughter couldn't confide in me. We had had mother-daughter talks about this and she had seen educational films at school about menstruation. She said that she thought I would be mad that she had soiled her panties. We had a talk about it and I showed her how to clean up her soiled panties, so if this happened in the future she would know what to do. Of course, now I completely understand why she felt ashamed and why she couldn't confide in me at the time. She felt very uncomfortable talking to me about sex.

Another thing that didn't seem right at the time involved an opened jar of marshmallow crème. The girls ate marshmallow crème on graham crackers as a snack on a regular basis. I kept a second jar under the stairwell in the basement. One day I found that jar opened and used. I assumed that the girls had been in the family room watching television, got hungry, and stuck their fingers in it instead of going upstairs to use the opened jar. This wasn't the case, though. A couple of years ago, I discovered that my husband placed the marshmallow crème on the head of his penis on the first day he had my daughter perform oral sex on him—just before she turned 8 years old. Never in my wildest imagination would I have ever dreamed that this was why the marshmallow crème was opened. That was the day he convinced her that she was his "special daughter" and that they shared a "special secret." There were many times I heard her tell her sister that *she* was "Daddy's special daughter."

The oldest daughter was his favorite. Everyone in the family knew this by the way he treated our youngest daughter. There's 25 months' difference in age between the girls. The oldest was the extrovert who always had to be busy playing with other children, and the youngest was the introvert who kept herself busy playing with her toys or coloring. As a baby she didn't feel comfortable unless I was in sight. As she grew older, she stayed around me most of the time. My husband picked on her and he rarely believed her side of the story when conflict arose between the two girls.

He was the third child in his family—the firstborn was a stillborn girl, the second a boy who died of a brain aneurysm at age 24. He and his brother were 4-1/2 years apart. He claimed that he always got his brother in trouble because he was the instigator when conflict developed. And since he was the youngest, his mother placed the responsibility on the oldest child, stating that he should have kept his little brother out of trouble. As a result of this childhood behavior pattern, he generally took the side of our oldest daughter. Even though he didn't believe in spanking children, he frequently slapped our youngest daughter in the back of the head. He didn't do this to our oldest daughter. It was rare at mealtime when we all sat down together that he didn't slap the youngest one in the head. Consequently, we had many arguments about the slapping, but no matter how much I protested, he still did it. I was afraid she would end up brain damaged. It was as though he went overboard disciplining our youngest daughter and neglected disciplining our oldest daughter.

When I look back, I realize that he went along with everything our oldest daughter wanted and everything she was interested in doing. His retort to me when I questioned him was, "What will it hurt?" I grew up knowing the word "no" and felt that every child should know that word and its meaning. In fact, I thought it wasn't good for a child not to know that there were boundaries and exactly what they were.

After the divorce, I took my oldest daughter, who was by now a teenager, to a psychologist because she had been stealing nonsense items from a little neighbor girl. My mother also told me at that time that my daughter stole things from her home and from my younger sister. The local Wal-Mart store watched her on camera because they suspected that she stole from them. When I asked her "Why?" she wouldn't look at me and answered, "I don't know." I believed her behavior was in retaliation for the divorce. The psychologist told me that my daughter had symptoms typical of a rape victim. At that time, my daughters were rarely around my father without someone else being there because I still didn't trust him. The only other male person I could even think of that she was around was her father. I mentioned this to my mother and she talked to my daughter for me. My mom said, "Honey, has your Daddy ever touched you in places where he shouldn't touch you?" My daughter adamantly replied, "Why Grandma, my Daddy wouldn't do anything like that!" It wasn't until later on that I found out that children won't tell unless repeatedly asked. Of course I denied any problems to my mother when one night my father tried to molest me. I fought him off and he beat me up, and then he was arrested. Children are too scared to tell the truth—the dark secret.

On the evening of July 4, 1990, my 18-year-old daughter shot and killed her father as he lay on the couch passed out from drinking. There were two shots——she remembers the first shot and what happened. She doesn't remember the second shot, the fatal shot through his temple. I truly believe it's because she was dissociating—distancing herself from the situation. This is what a renowned psychologist testified to. After examining and testing my daughter, the psychologist found that she had 14 symptoms typical of a rape victim. The doctor stated that my daughter felt the abuse was a vicious circle and there was no other way to escape from her father's torture, which she had endured since she was 8 years old. I honestly believe that she was programmed by her father to commit this act and that she is not a cold-blooded killer. All the years of tremendous confusion came to a head that night. She was found guilty of first-degree murder by a jury and is now serving a life sentence without parole in the state of Missouri.

My daughter is in the process of healing. Much of her healing has been through writing about the sexual abuse, finally telling about the first day it started, the first time she was raped, what he did to her, and how confused it all seemed to her while growing up. I retype her chapters onto diskettes and forward them for editing and submission to a publisher. Someday my daughter's story will be in print. It's very painful dredging up old memories both for her and for me, although writing her book actually helps both of us heal. Reading what she's written and knowing what I know from her childhood prove that the abuse happened.

My daughter gave me clues that the abuse was going on through her behavior while she was growing up. And, although I knew in the back of my mind that "something wasn't right," I couldn't figure out what troubled her so. Now I know and it's too late—the years of torture cannot be undone. I will not truly rest until my daughter is released. In a way, I now have my daughter back because the dark secret is out. We have an honest, open, loving, and caring relationship.

In conclusion, I can only emphasize that you should always question the little things that don't seem quite right. Go with your gut feelings. Listen to the signals that your child may be sending you. Be alert to negative behavior patterns that develop as your child becomes an adolescent. Educate yourself. Always keep the lines of communication open with your child. If you feel the least bit suspicious, take your child to a qualified doctor to be examined.

The cost of caring for maltreated children is $9 billion a year.

Source: (website) Georgia Council on Child Abuse, Inc. *The Statistics,* http://www.gcca.org/stat/index.html

ART THERAPY

COLETTE M. RICKERT, M.A.T., L.P.C.C., A.T.R.-BC

*I knew my child was dying inside. He'd been through so much. He'd been hit. He'd seen me hurt. A friend of his had been killed by a relative. I knew he'd been hurt a lot, but I didn't know how much for sure until I saw him draw this picture of a cemetery (**Figure 12-1**). I knew right then that the feeling I had inside of me about my child was true. He was drawing about his friend's death and wanting to kill one of the people who had hurt me so bad. But I knew inside of me that he was drawing how HE felt inside—like it was him who was dying. When I saw that picture, I knew inside of ME that I had to get him some help.*

This mother responded to feelings and intuitions "inside of her" that her child was in emotional pain and needed help with those feelings. During the course of therapy, her child was able to use art as a way to communicate about events he found to be too overwhelming verbally and emotionally to discuss. In the early stages of treatment, this child fluctuated between wild outbursts of energy and silent, deep depression. He often spent long periods of time making detailed drawings. His ability to discuss what bothered him was hampered by his inability to find the words he was looking for. Also, when he became extremely frightened or upset, his language often became offensive and inappropriate. The use of such language usually led to confrontations with people around him. As a result, the feelings that he was trying to communicate were often either misunderstood or not heard at all.

Figure 12-1. *The mother who discovered her young adolescent son drawing this picture said he described it as follows: "This is me killing [the person who hurt us]. His grave is ready for him and he won't hurt us anymore. I'm at the cemetery visiting my friend."*

When he came to art therapy, he found a valuable tool to help him relate what had happened both to him and to others that he loved. He was then able to avoid having his emotions overwhelm him and began to deal more effectively both mentally and emotionally with what he had experienced. Near the end of treatment, he was able to write a letter to his therapist **(Figure 12-2)**.

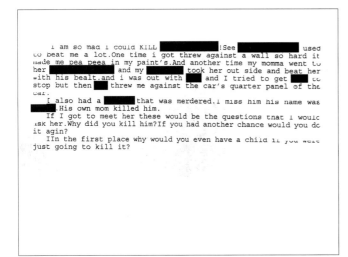

```
      i am so mad i could KILL ████████████!See ████████ used
to beat me a lot.One time i got threw against a wall so hard it
made me pea peea in my paint's.And another time my momma went to
her ████████ and my ████████ took her out side and beat her
with his bealt.and i was out with ██ and I tried to get ██ to
stop but then ██ threw me against the car's quarter panel of the
car.
      I also had a ████████ that was merdered.i miss him his name was
████████.His own mom killed him.
      If I got to meet her these would be the questions that i would
ask her.Why did you kill him?If you had another chance would you do
it agin?
      IIn the first place why would you even have a child if you were
just going to kill it?
```

Figure 12-2. *Letter from a child near the end of treatment.*

WHAT IS ART THERAPY?

Art therapy was established as a human service profession in the United States in 1969 when the American Art Therapy Association was formed. However, "the purposeful use of art" to help people in various mental and physical health settings began in the 1930s.

Making art can be very therapeutic. But making art is not the same as art therapy. Art used with and for therapy can be compared to exercise used with and for physical healing, or physical therapy. Doing exercise and doing art can help people feel better. But if there is a physical injury, then exercise used as part of a physical therapy program becomes an important part of the healing process. So, too, with art. If an injury has occurred to the mental, physical, emotional, or creative part of an individual, art can be used to help in the healing process.

The American Art Therapy Association (1996) defines art therapy as follows:

Art therapy is a human service profession that utilizes art media, images, the creative art process, and patient/client responses to the created products as reflections of an individual's development, abilities, personality, interests, concerns, and conflicts. Art therapy practice is based on knowledge of human development and psychological theories which are implemented in the full spectrum of models of assessment and treatment including educational, psychodynamic, cognitive, transpersonal, and other therapeutic means of reconciling emotional conflicts, fostering self-awareness, developing social skills, managing behavior, solving problems, reducing anxiety, aiding reality orientation, and increasing self-esteem.

EDUCATIONAL REQUIREMENTS FOR ART THERAPISTS

Art therapists are required to complete a master's degree in art therapy and have between 600 and 1000 hours of supervised practicum experience. After meeting these requirements, the art therapist can apply for registration. A registered art therapist (A.T.R.) is then eligible to take a written certification examination. After successfully passing this, the therapist is qualified as a board-certified art therapist (A.T.R.-BC). This credentialing is maintained by continuing education credits.

PARENTING AND PROTECTING CHILDREN

Being a parent can sometimes feel like an awesome responsibility. Raising a child successfully to adulthood is a full-time job. And manuals with directions for perfect assembly, maintenance, and use are hard to find!

Many books have been published on the best way to raise your child. A trip to your local library or bookstore can provide an armful of books filled with various helpful suggestions on what to do with or to your children to raise them in the best way possible. But although these books can be interesting and helpful, understanding the developmental stages a child moves through naturally can also provide ideas on how to raise children. Great joy can be experienced while watching them pass through these various stages. Behaviors that might otherwise seem confusing or irritating can become easier to understand and even possibly can be enjoyed as your child tries to build trust or strengthen their independence.

Knowing What to Expect Can Help

In addition to helping parenting be more enjoyable, knowing about the stages of development can add to your ability to protect your child. Because these stages are predictable, if you know the basic developmental tasks your child is facing and the artwork that is commonly produced in this stage, you can better spot warning signals that something may not be right.

Many parents feel like the mother at the beginning of this chapter: "I knew inside of me." Honoring feelings "inside" is one way parents protect their children. When your intuition is combined with your knowledge of development and artwork, you will pay more attention to the warning signs you see.

Stages of Early Development and Art

Experts have described children's developmental stages in various ways, but the following links artistic stages of growth with psychological development. Examples of common, average, and predictable drawings are shown here to provide you with an idea of what you can expect to see at the various stages. **Significant deviations or ongoing artwork that "doesn't feel right" can alert you that your child may be in danger or in need of outside help.**

Learning to trust. This stage begins at or before birth and continues until about age 18 months. Children try to make sense of the people and world around them. They spend most of their energy trying to learn what is in their environment and what feels safe and unsafe. At this point, children seem to believe the world revolves around them. And for anyone who has cared for a child of this age, it can feel like that to you, too!

Children's motor skills are usually too underdeveloped during these months to be able to create actual artwork. Smearing cereal, throwing dirt, pulling hair, and sucking on objects and fingers constitute most of their artistic expressions.

Becoming an individual. This stage begins at about 18 months of age and continues to about 36 months. During this time, children have experiences that lead them to believe that they may not be the center of the universe. In fact, if you observe a 2-year-old in the middle of a tantrum, it is easy to see the frustration experienced when the tasks or adventures the child desires are not allowed.

Children's muscles and motor skills are beginning to develop and they are trying to make sense of and take control of their world, their feelings, and themselves (for example, potty training). At this time in their life, they also begin to use scribbles (**Figure 12-3, a to d**) as building blocks to show and describe the world around them, just as they will later use the alphabet as building blocks for words in their reading and writing.

Belonging to a group, beginning to think, and I'm a boy/girl! Having gained a sense of who they are and some idea of how to control themselves in the world around them, children begin to venture out to learn how to interact with others and to intensely study and question what is going on in the world. This period of questioning and thinking is easily recognized because there is generally one repeated word—WHY? Children of this age have a tireless curiosity about people, places, and life itself. It is as if they are beginning to see the planet they are living on for the first time and they want to understand how the people and objects around them all fit together—and how they will fit in and function in the world (**Figure 12-4**).

Fig. 12-3a

Fig. 12-3b

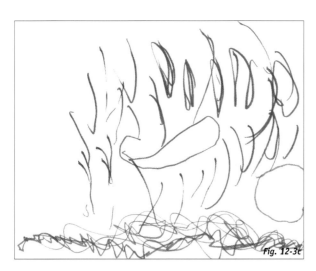

Fig. 12-3c

Fig. 12-3d

Figure 12-3. *Basic scribbles, ages 2 to 4 years.* **a,** *Two-year-old. Examples showing process of discovering and experimenting with the basic scribble shapes that will be the basis for all other artwork and writing.* **b,** *Three-year-old. Experiments with the basic scribble shapes and uses scribble lines and circles to form letters and words (Mom, Dad).* **c,** *Three-year-old. "It's raining on the ground."* **d,** *Four-year-old.*

Fig. 12-4a

Fig. 12-4b

Fig. 12-4c

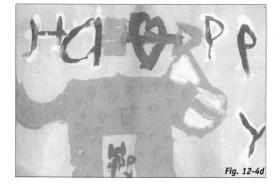

Fig. 12-4d

Figure 12-4.
*"Preschematic" drawings, ages 4 to 7 years. **a,** Four-year-old. Blending scribbles, lines, and shapes to draw a person. **b,** Four-year-old. Human figure with a circle used for the head and lines for the arms and legs. **c,** Four-year-old. "My friend Emily." **d,** Six-year-old. Painting of "A Happy Animal." **e,** Seven-year-old. "My Home in the Snow."*

Fig. 12-4e

Growing up some more. Between the ages of 7 and 12 years, the developmental stages that children have already passed through seem to be revisited, but at a slower pace and with more focused attempts to master them (**Figures 12-5 and 12-6**). You may find children seeking:

- Who can I trust (at school)?

- How am I going to control myself (on the playground)?

- Who will have lunch with me?

- Why do I have to do all of this homework?

- Why can't I go to the movies with my new friends?

- Who are my friends anyway?

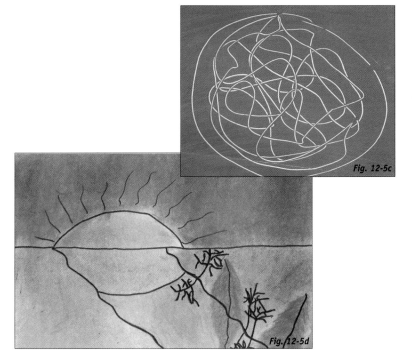

Figure 12-5. "Schematic" drawings, ages 7 to 9 years. ***a,*** Seven-year-old. "Mom and Dad's Chairs." The basic scribble shapes and lines are evolving into more defined objects and numbers. ***b,*** Eight-year-old. "Visitation." ***c,*** Eight-year-old. "Mandala." Basic scribble lines have become symbols and geometric lines. The child's self-assurance and definite ways of looking at things emerge, as shown by the full-bodied colors and distinctive lines that are created. ***d,*** Nine-year-old. "Camping Sunset." An awareness of the environment and how things fit together are shown in this drawing.

165

Fig. 12-6a

Fig. 12-6b

Fig. 12-6c

Figure 12-6. *Drawing realism, ages 9 to 11 years. **a,** Nine-year-old. "Raccoon." Basic scribble lines and circles have evolved into tools that can be used to emphasize details and try to be more realistic. **b,** Ten-year-old. "Bamboo Watercolor." Even while experimenting with watercolors, this child's artwork reflects a realistic depiction of bamboo. Basic scribble lines are part of the artwork, serving as natural markings to depict a lifelike image. **c,** Eleven-year-old. "Me." The artist's need to reflect on herself and her gender can be seen in this mask. Decorations appear at this age for the first time.*

And growing up the rest of the way to adulthood. From ages 13 to 18, the developmental task of children seems to be to get it all to work together. Body images seem to change daily. Nothing fits the way it used to—not clothes, not feelings, not friends, not ideas. You find them challenging you: *You can't tell me what to do! Why didn't you tell me what to do?* The struggle to gain control of themselves and their lives can feel overwhelming during this stage to both parents and children. It is easy to want to help, to want to straighten things out for them and to want to tell them what to do and ease their very apparent growing pains. But it is not that easy. Because it is their task to grow up, it is also their job to figure out how to put it all together. This doesn't mean that we as parents don't hurt with them when they fail, or rejoice with them when they are successful. **While their task is to refine their awareness, define their own direction, and confine their out-of-control urges and energies, our task is to stand by and be their coach, their mentor, and their guide (Figure 12-7, a to d).**

ART MATERIALS

Those who take care of children and interact with children, even if they aren't art therapists, can have available various art materials so that the child can easily find and use them. It is natural for children to want to explore and play with art materials, and this helps to create an environment that allows them to express themselves, even when words may be difficult. Art activities not only help the child achieve various developmental tasks, but also allow them to express their feelings about some of the complicated experiences they have.

Each person develops a personal way of thinking, speaking, walking, and dressing, and these individual characteristics eventually come to

Fig. 12-7a

Fig. 12-7b

Fig. 12-7c

Fig. 12-7d

Figure 12-7. *Adolescent drawings, ages 14 to 17 years. **a**, Seventeen-year-old. "Willy." Note the development and exaggeration of detail. **b**, Sixteen-year-old. "Christ." This is a subjective drawing of how this figure "feels" to the artist. Note the shading and the attempt to create a definite expression on the face. Basic scribble lines and shapes are completely evolved as tools to create an image with a purposeful intent, interpretation, and feeling. **c**, "Pseudo-naturalistic" drawing by a 13-year-old. "Still Life." There is greater attention to detail and objects that have a personal meaning. **d**, Another "pseudo-naturalistic" drawing, this one by a 14-year-old. "Winnie the Pooh." Cartooning is common at this age.*

be the way we know that person. The same is true of a child's creative expressions. When the child is permitted, he or she will develop a nonverbal system of symbols for self-expression. His or her dreams, feelings, thoughts, and experiences are then expressed in a particular way. Over time, parents learn to understand and communicate with the child on his or her creative level just as we learn to communicate with them verbally. If children do not feel "spied on" or criticized, they continue to express themselves creatively. Parents who pay attention to their child's drawings and other creations with sensitivity to the child's feelings will find a way of "hearing" what the child is actually saying. Then, if a problem exists or is developing, these parents who have learned to "listen" will hear and see what is happening.

If you expect your child to communicate with you at a deep and personal level, you must resist the urge to make yourself feel worthwhile by exerting control over your children. It is much more effective to focus on providing a safe, structured, and protective environment within which your children can grow and evolve their own ability to control themselves. The freedom to explore themselves is too often a luxury that children are not allowed to have. Instead, they are forced to use their creative energies to defend their individuality against parents and other adults—forces that are bigger and stronger physically, psychologically, mentally, and emotionally. This kind of controlling environment does not allow the child to try things that are different or to be creative in a way that fits his or her personality without feeling guilt and criticism.

Table 12-1 lists various art materials that you can keep available for children to use. It is important to provide materials that are appropriate for the child's age, interests, and ability level.

Table 12-1. Art Materials

Paper—all shapes, sizes, types	Plastic crayons
Old wallpaper books	Water pencils
Tissue from inside shoe boxes	Water crayons
Pencils	Water colors
Shoulder pads	Tempera paints
Popsicle sticks	Finger paints
Colored pencils	Brushes
Flour and water	Newspapers
Pipe cleaners	Boxes
Cray Pas	Fabrics
Traditional 8-1/2 x 11 or 11 x 14 sheets	Plasticine
Used wrapping paper	Beans
"Stuff"—anything that is interesting to touch or see	Beads
Clay	Nuts and bolts
Pens	Tape of all sizes and shapes
Construction paper	Old holiday cards
Small tree branches	Magazines and catalogs
Crayons	Paper towels or toilet paper rolls
Food coloring	Styrofoam boards (from food packages)
Stickers	Rubberbands
Pastels	Scissors
Markers	Buttons
Oil crayons	Glues of all colors and styles
	Thread and yarn

I Get the Feeling That Something Might Be Bothering My Child

When a child is maltreated, it affects his or her creative development as well as other aspects, making it difficult to move through the various developmental stages correctly. Often children become stuck at the stage where the abuse occurred, or they may regress consistently to that age when they express themselves in artwork. Well-treated children's creative development flows from stage to stage, always moving toward a more complete and more mature expression of themselves. But when victims of maltreatment try to create, they create from what they see, who they are, and where they have been, which is based on injury rather than good health. Children who are not mistreated and can explore their mental, emotional, physical, and spiritual aspects without fear learn to feel comfortable with themselves and where they fit in the world. Children who have to repress hurt, anger, etc., in order to survive are using their energy to protect and defend themselves. Their efforts to cope with stress are reflected in their art.

Examples of Drawings by Children Needing Help

Help with Adjusting to a New Sibling

Figure 12-8 was created by a very intelligent, first-born child. The arrival of a new baby in the home brought out the following reactions:

Figure 12-8. *Drawn by a 4-year-old dealing with the arrival of a new sibling.*

- Loud objection to any visitors to the home

- Remarks about who was actually going to be the baby's mother, indicating competitiveness

- Drawings

This drawing sums up the child's feelings about the new baby. The mother is shown in the upper left. The older sibling is below her, laying down like a baby. The new baby is drawn on the right as a large figure with four mouths. When she was asked about the picture, she said, "That's just how he is!"

By seeing how this older child felt about the new baby, the parents were able to adjust the way they interacted with her and help ease the transition to sharing her parents with the new sibling.

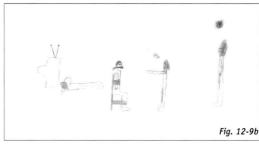

Fig. 12-9b

Fig. 12-9a

Figure 12-9, a and b.
*Drawings showing how the family is now **(a)** and how it would be with the stepfather **(b)**.*

Help with Adjusting to a New Stepparent

Even under the best of circumstances, marriage is challenging. Remarriage can intensify the challenge, and remarriages with children involved can sometimes feel like a military war game. Knowing that one of her children had uncomfortable feelings about a possible stepfather, the mother gave her the opportunity to sit with a therapist and discuss her fears and worries.

During the session, the therapist suggested drawing what the family was like now and what she thought would happen if there was a stepfather in the house. **Figures 12-9, a and b** are from that session. In the drawing of how the family is now (Figure 12-9, *a*), the youngest child is watching television, the child drawing is getting ready to ride her bike and play with her team, and the oldest child is drawn as the star of the family. On the far left, the mother is shown with a question mark over her head, indicating that she is confused. The people in the drawing are full figures and all four have smiles on their faces. In contrast, Figure 12-9, *b* shows what the child thought it would be like if her mother remarried and a stepfather was living with them. The youngest child is still watching television but he has his back to the rest of the family. The oldest child has disappeared and only quotation marks remain around the space where the oldest child was in the first drawing. The mother is standing behind the child who drew the picture and is yelling at her. The child has drawn herself standing in front of the stepfather, who is tied up to a chair and gagged. She is pointing at him and laughing. All of the original family members are drawn much thinner or gone, except the youngest child. The child drawing the picture shows herself as mocking the potential stepparent.

Seeing how this child felt helped give the engaged couple a clear picture of what was bothering the child. They were then able to address the problem and plan for how power and power issues could be approached. The potential stepparent did not want to intrude on this family and remained quiet. The child interpreted this soft and passive behavior as weakness; she was concerned that she would "run him over" and "another marriage would be ruined because of the fighting."

Fig. 12-10b

Help with Healing from Abuse

Fig. 12-10a

The child who drew **Figures 12-10, a and b** had experienced several physical and psychological episodes of abuse both personally and by seeing people he cared about be abused. He was brought to the art therapist for help in the healing process.

Figure 12-10, a and b.
Drawings showing the child's "bad" (a) and "good" (b) sides.

When he was asked about himself, he said he was "good and bad." He was asked to draw a picture showing "his good" and "his bad." Figure 12-10, *a* shows "his bad"—represented by a devil figure. Figure 12-10, *b* shows "his good"—represented by an angel. The proportions of the figures accurately reflected his feelings about himself. This child also drew his good part on the back of the paper with his bad part. He said that he did this because it was just like him—"I put the bad side on top where people see it in case I have to fight with them. I don't show the good side because they'd just cream me!" Part of the therapy focused on helping him balance his "good and bad" more evenly—with both on top so that people could see the good side as well as the bad.

Fig. 12-11a

Help in Dealing with the Past

Figures 12-11, a and b are part of a much larger group of drawings created from therapy sessions and gathered from childhood scrapbooks. The client entered into therapy feeling extremely depressed and having suicidal thoughts but not having any idea of what was bothering him.

He created Figure 12-11, *a* as a part of a series designed to help him understand why he felt so hopeless and depressed. There is a faded house in the background and a man's head mounted on a stick and attached to a vehicle. He created Figure 12-11, *b* as a card for his mother on Mother's Day. It shows an outlined child's hand with painted nails and a butterfly ring.

Fig. 12-11b

Figure 12-11, a and b.
Drawings that indicate a need for help from the past.

The man said he found the first picture to be "odd," but after discussing it further and spending time in therapy and looking at things that he had created as a child, he began to tie together pieces of information about various physical and sexual abuse that he had experienced. Eventually he understood that his mother had desperately wanted a little girl, creating trauma for him. This trauma resulting from her desire was so intense that by the time he became an adult, he had learned to completely separate himself from identifying with his body, his feelings, and his thoughts, so that he did not feel the pain of rejection. He began to see that his thoughts of suicide were linked to his mother's deep desire for him to either be a girl or disappear completely.

Help with Finding Out What is Wrong

Sometimes we as parents have that uncomfortable "inside feeling" that something is bothering our child or that something has happened but the child either cannot or has not mentioned any particular problem. Over time, if the child produces a significant number of drawings that make you "not feel right," these can be signals that the child is in need of help.

The sample drawings shown here (**Figures 12-12 to 12-20**) are part of a series brought in by a concerned parent. The child had created them both in and out of school; some represented subjects assigned by the teacher and others were spontaneous creations. They were drawn over a 5-month period of time. Drawings that the child had done previously had been appropriate for the child's age and stage of development. The parent was concerned that the child was experiencing too much stress in a family-related area. Despite the child's ability to create artwork that accurately expressed feelings and trauma related to the situation, it was not until much later that the child was able to tell about what the problem was.

USING ART IN THE THERAPY PROCESS

Art reflects various inner feelings and ideas as well as various stages and ages in our lives. The series of drawings (**Figures 12-21 to 12-24**) shown here were done in a 15-minute period of time by a 5-year-old who had come to his therapy session extremely upset and angry. The only words he said when he arrived were, "No," and "You can't make me." This language is typical of a 2-year-old who is trying to deal with difficult feelings.

After the boy's tantrum and having drawn these pictures, he was able to regain his composure, talk about what was bothering him, and leave the session feeling relaxed.

Figure 12-12. *"A Sad Cat."*

Figure 12-13. *"An Empty Bench."*

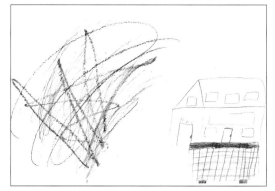

Figure 12-14.
"My Home."

Figure 12-15. *"Me."*

Figure 12-16.
"Outside."

Figure 12-18. *"Coloring Book Page."*

Figure 12-17. *"Night and Day."*

Figure 12-19. *"Bangeled Tiger."*

Figure 12-20. *"Watercolor of House."*

Figure 12-21. *"A Scribble." This is typical of a 2-year-old. After this, the child grabbed a piece of paper and crunched it after promising he would draw a picture––behavior very typical of a 2-year-old.*

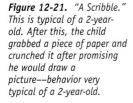

Figure 12-22. *"Another Scribble." This scribble is smaller and has a circle in the middle with a more shaded area. This is more typical of a child moving into the preschematic stage, ages 4 to 7 years.*

Figure 12-23. *"More Scribbles." This drawing is more open and almost appears to take on a shape. The basic scribbles lines and circles are more organized than in the earlier two drawings.*

Figure 12-24. *"The Volcano in Me." The child had calmed himself and began putting his energy into the drawing. Although the organization is not perfect, the picture shows that the child's perspective and self-control are greatly improved. This is a picture of the volcano inside of him that explodes. There are four trees firmly planted in the ground as well as the ground itself. This is much more age-appropriate for a 5-year-old child.*

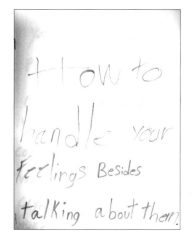
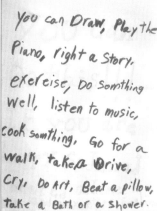
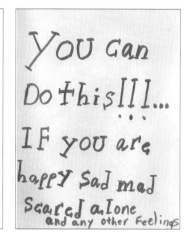

Figure 12-25. *Pages from a child telling how to handle feelings.*

CONCLUDING THOUGHTS

Artwork can help the child express his or her need for help. As a parent, you need to pay attention to your intuition, that "feeling inside" that tells you something may be wrong. You should also pay attention if your child produces a significant amount of disturbing artwork over a long period of time (Figure 12-25).

If you need assistance in finding an art therapist, you can contact the American Art Therapy Association, Inc. at the following address:

> *1202 Allanson Road*
> *Mundelein, IL 60060*

Or you can call (847) 949-6064 or FAX them at (847) 566-4580.

SUGGESTED READINGS

Adamson, E.: *Art as Healing,* London: Coventure Ltd., 1984.

American Art Therapy Association, Inc.: *Information and Membership,* The Association.

Dalley, T.: *Art as Therapy: An Introduction to the Use of Art as a Therapeutic Technique,* New York: Tavistock Publications, 1984.

Gardner, H.: *Artful Scribbles: The Significance of Children's Drawings,* 1980.

Kellogg, R.: *Analyzing Children's Art,* 1970.

Kellogg, R.: *Children's Drawings, Children's Minds,* New York: Avon Books, 1979.

Lowenfeld, V., and Brittain, W.L.: *Creative and Mental Growth,* 7th edition, New York: Macmillan Publishing Co., Inc., 1982.

Rubin, J.A.: *Child Art Therapy: Understanding and Helping Children Grow Through Art,* New York: Litton Education Publishing, Inc., 1978.

Ulman, E., Kramer, E., and Kwiatkowska, H.Y.: *Art Therapy in the United States,* Craftsbury Common, VT: Art Therapy Publications, 1978.

Woollams, S., Brown, M., Huige, K.: *Transactional Analysis in Brief,* Ann Arbor, Michigan: Huron Valley Institute, 1976.

Nearly two-thirds of child abuse reports come from professional sources— education, social services, law enforce- ment, medicine.

Source: U.S. Department of Health and Human Services. *Child Maltreatment 1996: Reports from the States to the National Child Abuse and Neglect Data System*, Washington, D.C.: U.S. Government Printing Office, 1998.

PREVENTION OF ABUSE

PEGGY S. PEARL, ED. D.

Keeping your children safe takes you and everyone your child comes into contact with working together. An old African saying, "It takes a village to raise a child," reflects the level of safety and security that parents need to provide for their children. The truth in this saying appears clear and simple. But it begs the question: What is a "child- and family-friendly" village or community?

It takes more than "a successful child abuse prevention program" to keep children safe. It takes a society and a community that value their children. It takes a community that is willing to be proactive by funding preventive services, programs, and policies rather than one that focuses on being reactive by attempting to solve the crises caused when these services are unavailable. The central goal of child abuse prevention is providing all parents with the necessary resources for successful parenting. **Table 13-1** lists indicators of a nation that places a high priority on its children.

SOCIETY'S COMMITMENT TO CHILDREN

The first step in preventing child abuse is the commitment by society to its children and the prevention of their maltreatment. This commitment can be seen when society's leaders activate initiatives to support families and children. This leadership must come from both the public and the private sectors.

Although government can play a critical role in ensuring the public health and safety of its citizens, we cannot assume that child abuse prevention is only a function of government. The private sector must assume a role in supporting families in the work place and in supporting community-wide efforts on behalf of children. **Family-friendly work place policies include job sharing, flextime, mental health care, medical and dental insurance, parental leave,**

employee assistance programs, and dependent-care assistance programs. In particular, unemployment creates circumstances that are high risk for child abuse and neglect. Effective job training, placement, and full employment are among the important elements in a society's ongoing commitment to children.

Table 13-1. Indicators of a Nation with Children as a High Priority
Outraged citizens are motivated to action when they hear that children are being maltreated.
Adequate and affordable housing is available for all families.
Recreation and esteem-building activities are available to all children and families.
Mental health, medical, and dental care are accessible to all families.
Social service delivery systems are used by families in need of assistance before maltreatment occurs rather than relying on systems that treat after abuse occurs or punish for maltreating.
Universal instruction in the care and guidance of children is found in the curriculum of all public and private schools (kindergarten through twelfth grade and adult continuing education programs).
Instruction in interpersonal communications, nonviolent conflict resolution, and resource management is provided to all students (kindergarten through twelfth grade and adult continuing education programs).
Job training and education programs provide all workers with access to jobs as an avenue out of poverty.
Work place policies support families and include parental leave, job sharing, flextime, employee assistance programs, dependent-care assistance programs, mental health care, medical and dental insurance, career ladders, and employee wellness programs.
Nonviolent societal role models are highly visible.
All parents have access to self-help and support groups. Adequate funding exists for research to build the database concerning what environments provide for the optimal development of individuals throughout the life span.
Legal systems, both criminal and civil, are properly funded, staffed, and trained to promptly and fairly resolve maltreatment cases.
Culturally and ethnically sensitive home-based parent education programs are available to all new parents.
Adequate salaries are provided for professionals who work in all child-related professions so that agencies are able to attract and retain the best and the brightest in jobs caring for the nation's priority—children and their families.

The Role of the Media

The different forms of media play an important role in shaping public opinion about children and, in turn, the attitudes concerning child abuse and neglect. The media, which sells its column inch and air time to advertisers to change the behavior of consumers, must accept the fact that it is accountable for the types of programs presented. The goal should be to provide prudent and responsible programming that does not accept and glamorize violence. This behavior-shaping role can be critical in helping to create a public opinion that will not tolerate violence in any form. The media can help parents and teachers teach nonviolent conflict resolution. The media has been involved in, and should continue to be involved in, educating the public concerning the presence of violence in the lives of families, what its consequences are, and possible alternatives. Some things that the media can do are to:

- Reduce the amount of violence portrayed in programming for all family members.

- Become an advocate for policies beneficial to children and families.

- Portray parenting as an important and valued job in our society.

Along with other sectors, the media should help to create a broader sense of community and take seriously its role in preparing our future leaders—our children.

Providing Parenting Information and Support

Within a society, basic prevention programs should be available to all parents *before* maltreatment begins. All parents need access to parenting information, especially when their first babies are born. Perinatal coaching, home visitor, and parent aide programs have proven effective for parents with young children (see discussion of programs for new parents, p. 183). In addition, all parents need access to health care both for themselves and for their children.

Parent education classes should be accessible to all parents as part of a comprehensive adult education program in every community. Topics covered should include principles of child development (where the parents are given information about what is normal in a child's development and what is not), positive child guidance techniques (including discipline, role-modeling, and handling emotions), and basics in child care (such as child nutrition and safety instruction). Classes for parents with children of all ages should teach techniques to improve parent-child interactions. Learning to play with and enjoy their children enhances the parent-child interaction and increases the parents' enjoyment of their role as a parent. Child guidance techniques, an area of high risk for possible abuse, should emphasize relationship building rather than rules.

All parents need stress management training and access to positive support services to help them cope with the stresses of parenting. One way grandparents and other relatives and friends can help is to offer to take care of children when they notice that the parents are stressed—or simply in need of a break. In our highly mobile society, many families lack the positive support that can come from family and friends. Consequently, they need support from other sources such as the church, social organizations, or mental health agencies. Families, including single parents and those classified as "working poor," also need accessible and affordable child care so that they can continue to work and not worry constantly about what is going on with their children.

Corporal punishment can easily become abusive when it is administered by parents, caregivers, or teachers who are angry and under stress. Therefore all parents and caregivers require instruction in the positive methods of child guidance. Self-help groups such as Parents Anonymous (PA) give parents alternatives to abusing, emotionally or physically, their children as well as positive support networks of individuals and other parents where they can turn for support. This should help keep abusive patterns from beginning as well as help stop abusive behaviors that have begun. PA uses the Alcoholics Anonymous (AA) model of self-help. All parents must have access to support groups that offer both primary prevention (stopping the abuse before it begins) and tertiary prevention (working to develop more constructive ways of coping once the abusive pattern is interrupted). Therefore parents who use positive child guidance techniques can benefit by enhancing both their own and their child's self-esteem.

Where can parents go to find such training? Sources include:

- Hospitals, which provide ongoing family wellness programs

- Junior colleges that offer either a curriculum in child care professions or that have a program of evening adult education courses

- High schools that offer evening adult education courses or ongoing parent education for parents of their students

- Churches that have programs to train babysitters

- Companies that offer employee assistance programs

- Scouting organizations that offer training in various leadership roles

- National organizations (YMCA, YWCA, the American Red Cross) that support family values and offer classes or seminars on child safety, disciplining children, building self-esteem, etc.

New Parent Programs

To enhance parenting and to prevent child abuse, all new parents can benefit from various instructional and support services. The specific content and structure of these programs will vary, as will the sponsoring agency or institution; however, the goals for such programs for new parents should include:

1. Increasing a parent's knowledge of child development and the demands of parenting

2. Enhancing a parent's skill in coping with the stresses of infant and child care

3. Enhancing parent-child bonding, emotional ties, and communication

4. Increasing a parent's skills in coping with the stress of caring for children with special needs

5. Increasing a parent's knowledge about how to manage a home and children

6. Reducing the burden of child care by providing respite for the family—times when the parent(s) can get away for a break

7. Increasing the access to social and health services for all family members

These programs are also offered by the organizations listed on page 182. New parents are often provided with brochures of information upon leaving the hospital with their newborn.

Parenting Skills Enhancement

Parent education must be available for parents who want to improve their parenting skills. Group-parent education programs, emphasizing impulse control and alternative methods of discipline, are particularly successful with physically abusive parents. One-to-one, home-based services built around individual counseling and problem-solving techniques are effective with neglectful parents. Neglectful parents especially need instruction in concrete child care tasks, such as diapering and feeding an infant, or distracting and communicating with a 2-year-old. The successful prevention of emotional abuse includes group-based services that define nonphysical methods of discipline; emphasize the need for consistency in determining and enforcing rules; and offer parents ways of demonstrating affection toward their children.

These group-based programs are often offered by school districts and are specific to a child's stage of development. Thus a parent of a child in the primary grades (1 to 3) may be able to attend a session on how to help his or her child in doing math homework—a source of frustration in this age group. Parents of middle school-aged children (grades 6 to 8) may be offered courses in building self-esteem in adolescents, who traditionally suffer low self-esteem linked to the many changes they are undergoing.

Principles Affecting Child Maltreatment

As this book shows, child maltreatment takes many forms and includes more than the obvious inflicted physical injury or sexual abuse. It is also verbally assaulting children and/or failing to meet their emotional needs, failing to provide adequate supervision, and neglecting or failing to provide food, clothing, shelter, and medical care. Physical abuse and verbal assault often result from parental stress and/or a lack of knowledge concerning child growth and development. Neglect usually results from parental poverty, substance abuse, and/or mental illness. All types of abuse are more common in families where parents were victims of some type of maltreatment.

The different types of child maltreatment share common causes. Therefore the ways that the society approaches child abuse and neglect prevention must try to impact as many causes of maltreatment as possible. However, we want to make specific mention of the programs to prevent neglect and sexual abuse, since the causes of these types of maltreatment differ slightly from the causes of physical and emotional abuse.

Preventing neglect. There is an income level under which parents cannot provide the necessary food, shelter, clothing, mental health, medical, and dental care for their children. At this poverty level of existence, parents also experience additional stress if adequate support systems are not in place. Currently in our society many individuals are employed full time at jobs that do not pay enough to provide the money to meet their children's basic needs. Many more parents lack the job skills necessary for even entry-level jobs. In addition, most entry-level jobs do not provide any medical and dental insurance. For a further challenge, our society's national and state governments are providing fewer mental health, medical, and dental services to citizens. These trends produce growing numbers of children who are without adequate mental health, medical, and dental care. When a society values its children and makes their welfare a priority, it seeks to ensure, by various public and private means, that all parents have access to the basic resources to care for their children. To care for our society's children, all parents need access to the following:

• Decent and affordable housing

• Adequate mental health services, medical care, and dental care

• Nutritious food

• Developmentally appropriate child care

The cycle of poverty, which contributes heavily to family disintegration and chronic violence, must be interrupted with effective programs that are oriented toward providing housing, jobs, substance abuse treatment, and family support. Programs can be found at the local levels through churches, food pantries, or crisis nurseries. Parents must seek and use such resources to provide adequately for their families.

To prevent neglect, parents also need to be functioning at optimal levels so they can focus on their children's needs. Many parents are unable to parent effectively because they have substance abuse or mental health problems. To prevent child maltreatment, these adults must have access to substance abuse prevention and treatment programs as well as mental health services so they will be able to function at their best each and every day. These services should be available to all parents either free, at fees based on ability-to-pay sliding scales, in a way covered by employee insurance, or through employee assistance programs.

Preventing sexual abuse. In the last decade, many sexual abuse prevention programs were developed and put into place, often being presented as a part of safety training in elementary schools. In most cases, these sexual abuse prevention programs taught children how to protect themselves from abuse. Researchers and clinicians caution, however, that the major responsibility for the prevention of sexual abuse cannot be placed on the victims and potential victims, since they are children. More sexual abuse prevention programs must focus on the adult, the perpetrator. The National Committee for the Prevention of Child Abuse has developed a comprehensive strategy to prevent adults from becoming child sexual abusers. Their prevention strategy includes those areas listed in **Table 13-2.**

Comprehensive child sexual abuse prevention strategies, like all prevention programs, strengthen individuals and families by enhancing parenting.

The National Committee for the Prevention of Child Abuse adds that when child sexual abuse programs or empowerment programs are used, they will only be effective for school-aged children if they are:

- Offered on the child's developmental level

- Presented by a parent or someone the child knows and trusts

- Repeated periodically

- Focused on stressing specific actions that the child can take to keep himself or herself safe

Table 13-2. Prevention Strategies

Strategy	Description
Education for adolescents and young children	Providing all adolescents with quality sex education, including healthy sexuality, during the preteen and teenage years to enhance their knowledge of what is normal and abnormal.
Training for professionals and volunteers who work with children	Teaching these individuals how to identify and help children who are being abused, how to teach children to protect themselves from abuse, and how to detect those who may be potential molesters.
Education for parents	Providing all new parents with quality education and support to enhance early attachment and bonding when their first babies are born, including information about appropriate and inappropriate touch and what to do about it as well as how to detect and handle symptoms in their children that may indicate that sexual abuse has occurred.
Institutional changes	Ensuring that all child-serving institutions and programs (schools, boys' clubs, Girl Scouts, daycare, etc.) train children in self-awareness and self-protection; putting guidelines and regulations in place to screen, train, and monitor all volunteers and staff; encouraging institutions to design their physical environments to provide openness and visibility within the facility to prevent any staff or volunteer from having the opportunity to be alone, unseen, or unsupervised with a child.
Media messages	Media should be encouraged to change the type of programming that is put on, especially putting less emphasis on aggression and violence; creating an environment in which prevention programs and concepts can be effective can communicate several messages to adults: • Child sexual abuse is a crime. • There is help available. • Abuse is a chronic problem unless you get help. • Children get hurt when you sexually abuse them. • Children cannot consent to sexual misbehavior. And messages to children: • It's OK to say no. • It's not your fault. • Reach out for help if this happens to you. • Help is available for you.

Chapters 3 and 4 tell how child sexual abusers condition, bribe, and/or threaten, terrorize, or coerce children not to tell. Abusers condition children to accept the maltreatment, then they become friends, and they manipulate the child. These adults are not easy to refuse or to tell on. Therefore sexual abuse prevention programs often fail to prevent sexual abuse or are ineffective in getting children to tell an adult about the abuse. Children should not be expected to protect themselves any more than any victim of assault, rape, or robbery can be expected to protect himself or herself. It takes parents, other adults, and a total society working together to be effective.

You should note that child sexual abuse prevention programs are not recommended for preschool children. Preschool children have not yet developed the necessary reasoning ability. They need appropriate adult supervision at all times, esteem-building activities, good communication skills, and general knowledge about their bodies.

Providing children with life skills education. All children need instruction in private or public schools regarding positive ways to interact with others as much as they need instruction in math, English, and science. Life skills education should be integrated into the curriculum beginning in pre-kindergarten and continuing into adult education. Life skills education includes those areas listed in **Box 13-1.** Note that some skills are appropriate for all ages and some are geared to the adult who will be dealing with children.

Box 13-1. Life Skills Education Areas

Nonviolent conflict resolution—working things out peacefully.

Stress management skills—using techniques that reduce stress.

Resource management—learning to ask for help and where to go to find it.

Decision-making—using critical thinking to evaluate situations and respond appropriately.

Interpersonal communication—getting along with others.

Specific skills in child development and guidance—learning what to expect, how to respond, and what is appropriate and inappropriate guidance for children.

Basics of substance abuse prevention education—focusing on how to say no and how to develop healthy self-esteem.

KNOWLEDGE IS POWER

Knowledge about the dangers in this world does not create paranoid children. Knowledge creates children who are self-confident and who feel in control of themselves, especially if the knowledge is accompanied by some idea of what to do in case they find themselves in a potentially dangerous situation. The information must be presented in words that children clearly understand and must be repeated as the child grows older. The child also needs to feel free to ask questions of parents and other adults at any time. Children readily sense when parents are nervous and anxious about a subject (see Chapter 6 for tips on communicating with children). When teaching children about personal safety, we must present the information in a matter-of-fact way—the same way we would teach children to watch for cars when crossing the street, to swim with a buddy, or not to play with matches.

Books are helpful in putting parents at ease so that they can talk about difficult subjects, especially sex. In addition to the books listed here, you should consult the list in **Box 13-2.**

- *The Body Book* by Claire Rayner (Piccolo Press) is an excellent book for children 3 to 12 years of age and their parents. It has great illustrations with simple explanations.

- Michelle Elliot's book *Feeling Happy, Feeling Safe* is a colorful picture book to help children from 3 to 7 years cope with bullies, strangers, getting lost, and advances from unknown adults.

Children with disabilities are at high risk for maltreatment. *The Disabled Child and Child Abuse,* by Donald F. Kline, from the Minnesota Committee for the Prevention of Child Abuse, 123 East Grant St., Minneapolis, MN 55403 is a useful resource for parents of children with special needs.

Parents have many tools for giving children information to keep them safe. For the "computer whiz kids," there is Macintosh and IBM computer software on personal safety.

- Continental Press, Elizabethtown, PA 17022-2299 (800 233-0759), offers *SMARTteam,* Part 1 Managing Anger and Part 2 Resolving Conflict. This software is designed for children in grades 5 to 9.

- For grades 6 to 12, there is *Body Awareness Resource Network (BARN),* a motivational, interactive program that shows students how to make safe, healthy choices.

These nonjudgmental programs present valuable information to older children. Activities that build self-esteem and improve knowledge about self-protection give children of all ages the confidence that makes them less easily victimized.

Box 13-2. Children's Books on Personal Safety

Gordon, S., & Gordon, J. (1987). *A Better Safe than Sorry Book.* Ed-UPress: New York. (3 to 9 year olds)

Hindman, J. (1985). *A Very Touching Book . . . for Little People and for Big People.* McClure-Hindman Associates: New York.

Kaufman, G., & Raphael, L. *Stick Up for Yourself!* Kidsrights: Charlotte, N.C. (8 to 13 year olds)

McFarland, R. (1995). *Copying Through Assertiveness.* Continental Press: Elizabeth, PA. (Teens)

Patterson, C., & Quiter, L. *Almost Grown-Up.* Kidsrights: Charlotte, NC. (For preteens–book on puberty and sexual development)

Planned Parenthood of Snohomish County, *It's My Body* with parent's guide, Planned Parenthood of Snohomish County: Evertt, WA 98201 (Preschool, early elementary).

My Personal Safety Coloring Book, Pridely Police Department, 6431 University Avenue N. E. Fridley, MN 55432. (Elementary age)

Peacemaker's Conflict Resolution Chart. Redleaf Press: St. Paul, MN.

Red Flag, Green Flag People, Rape and Abuse Crisis Center, P. O. Box 1655, Fargo, ND, 58101 (Preschool, early elementary)

Wochter, O. (1983). *No More Secrets for Me.* Little Brown, & Co.: Boston, MA. (Elementary age)

My Very Own Book About Me. Super Kids, R.C.N., Lutheran Social Services of Washington, N1226, Spokane, WA 99201. (Preschool, early elementary)

Marvel Comics, *Spiderman.* A series of comics. Spiderman talks about preventing sexual abuse as well other types of abuse. National Committee for the Prevention of Child Abuse: Chicago, IL.

Sweet, P. E., (1981). *Something Happened to Me.* Mother Courage Press: Racine, WI.

King County Rape Relief, (1984). *He Told Me Not to Tell* (pamphlet). *Top Secret: Sexual Assault Information for Teenagers Only.* King County Rape Relief, 305 South 43rd, Renton, WA 98055.

PREVENTION OF EMOTIONAL MALTREATMENT

The most common type of abuse is emotional abuse. Words can hurt more than paddles and can have life-long effects. Emotional abuse strips away layers of self-esteem, a fundamental ingredient in achieving a full and enriched life.

Each child is unique, and what may be simple correction for one may constitute abuse for another. For some children, a parent's words or tone of voice may be inappropriately harsh. To another child, the same words may be neutral or OK. Do we as parents or do other caregivers recognize the difference? Do we know what is appropriate based on the child's developmental level? Do we regularly or systematically, either publicly or privately, ridicule or demean our child? Do we, as parents, or as scout leaders, or perhaps as teachers, set standards that take into account the child's developmental level? Putting too much pressure on children to perform at levels for which they are not developmentally ready can easily make them think that they are not OK when they are, in fact, performing in accordance with their own developmental level. Applying too much pressure and teasing children for normal behavior affects their self-esteem negatively and makes them feel that they are not good enough.

Stop and think: *A scout leader ridicules a child's choice of clothing to him or her in front of the group, saying, "Are you really going to wear that on our outing?" How does it make the child feel when he or she may have made the decision based on a personal preference or on a special emotional attachment to that shirt?*

Stop and think: *How does it make a pre-teen boy feel when you as an adult make fun of his changing voice or other physical changes? How does he feel when you make light of his questions about changes in his body? Pre-teens, or children of any age, feel confused and "abnormal" when their bodies change. Adult humor and sarcasm are often misunderstood as being comments that are "making fun of" by pre-teens.*

Stop and think: *A young soccer player is having fun playing and watching his teammates play, when suddenly an adult yells, "If you can't play any better than that, get out of the game and let someone in who can play, dummy!" How would he feel?*

What adults say may have a long-term impact on the self-esteem of children. The words of adults are important to children, so we as adults have a responsibility to make sure the words are encouraging, sensitive, and positive. All adults who work with children can make a significant contribution in this area.

SAFETY IN CHILD CARE SITUATIONS
Screening and Training for Workers

Child care facilities present special challenges in the effort to prevent child maltreatment and to promote the welfare of children. For children to be safe, both volunteers and paid staff must be carefully screened and trained in the appropriate ways to interact with children. Agencies must routinely check criminal records as well as child abuse and neglect hotline records for all individuals who work with children. An even more important step to take is to have a knowledgeable professional interview each individual child care worker to screen for indicators of possible abusive behavior. The national offices of many youth-serving agencies have carefully researched effective screening methods and can assist other educational, service, recreational, and social service agencies. These national groups include Big Brothers/Big Sisters and the Boy Scouts of America. These organizations are searching for mentally healthy individuals who have a positive reason for wanting to donate their time to be with children. The Boy Scouts organization goes one step further, requiring co-leaders and encouraging parental involvement.

Many individuals who work with children one-on-one lack group management skills or an understanding of individual differences. These deficiencies hamper their ability to work effectively with a group of children. Parents need to observe how individuals such as coaches or scout leaders interact with their child(ren). Review the questions in **Table 13-3.** Volunteers or paid staff who fail to routinely demonstrate the positive characteristics that are listed are potential sources of psychological abuse—guilty of hitting children with negative words, insults, and excessive pressure to meet inappropriate and/or rigid adult standards. To prevent problems in these areas, we as parents need to get involved, especially by offering assistance or seeking assistance from appropriate supervisory sources, for example, administrative offices of scouting organizations. Individuals working with groups of children, especially volunteers, usually welcome training, support, and assistance. We as parents can support them by recognizing their positive contributions and efforts to grow as role models.

Table 13-3. Behaviors to Observe

Does the individual:

Share your child-rearing practices and values or impose their own?

Give your child positive feedback and guidance or merely tell your child what not to do?

Enjoy time and activities with your child and other children or appear to feel obligated to be there?

Have an appropriate sense of humor or use sarcasm and make fun of individuals, their actions, or their beliefs?

Give children guidance and choices or demand conformity to rigid rules?

Teach children negotiating skills to solve differences or routinely intervene with rigid dictates of what to do?

Appear relaxed and at ease or rushed, anxious, hurried, and/or preoccupied?

Set appropriate standards or pressure children to succeed at an adult standard?

Accept each child as an individual and allow for individual differences or demand uniformity and ridicule differences?

Appear to be someone your child likes to spend time with, someone your child fears or feels anxious around, or someone your child tries excessively to please?

Providing Supervision

Children of all ages need supervision by competent caregivers to keep them safe from accidents and abuse by peers, adolescents, and adults. The type of supervision that is required depends on the child's age and developmental level. For various reasons, some children are left unsupervised at ages that are too young for safety. These children or young teens are then free to experiment with drugs, sex, and other high-risk behaviors.

Before- and after-school supervision is important for pre-teens and some adolescents. The supervisory program may be recreational, cultural, or educational, but the result will be an appropriate use of the young person's time and talent. Providing young people with the opportunity to do volunteer work both boosts their self-esteem and teaches many important life concepts and skills. Intergenerational volunteer work may be especially valuable to children who do not have regular contact with grandparents or preschool children. There is also long-term value in having young people interact routinely with people who are different from themselves—people of different races, economic backgrounds, with physical or mental challenges, or from different cultures. The interaction reduces stereotyping and prejudice in addition to giving the individual a unique source of social interaction and the positive feelings that accompany helping someone else. A combination of activities may extend a child's or teen's knowledge and experience as well as keep them safely under adult supervision. For example, each day after school a teen could alternate helping inner-city children with reading, taking computer classes, helping with art or drama classes, leading a gymnastics class, swimming, or playing baseball. This would be a positive alternative to spending hours watching television, eating junk food, experimenting with drugs (alcohol or tobacco), or just "feeling sorry for yourself." It is healthy to have pre-teens and teens focus on others rather than themselves. And an additional value is that the habits formed during these important years will last a lifetime.

PARENTS AS ADVOCATES IN THE LEGAL SYSTEM

Comprehensive child abuse prevention includes prevention within the judicial system. Within the legal system, which includes the criminal, civil, and juvenile courts, there are laws and procedures to ensure the protection of children and support for families. But all judicial procedures should be sensitive to the needs of children and families. In addition, there must be adequate numbers of well-trained judges, lawyers, and court support staff, along with manageable caseloads, to handle the complex and demanding nature of child abuse and neglect litigation. The legal system should also be sensitive to the needs of victims of abuse, taking steps to prevent additional maltreatment of these vulnerable individuals within the system as well as protecting the child from a return to a dysfunctional, abusive family. To continually monitor the effectiveness of the legal and protective service systems, each community should have a citizen advocacy group in place. Citizen advocacy groups continually work to make sure that the policies of private and public sectors are the most effective and appropriate for both families and children. As parents, we must take part in the advocacy process by:

- Serving in the group

- Attending meetings held by the group

- Staying alert to situations in our communities and informing the group so that appropriate action can be taken

- Volunteering to take part in programs implemented by the citizen advocacy team

CONCLUDING THOUGHTS

To keep children safe is a universal concern of parents. We are shocked by news media reports of kidnapping, child abuse, drive-by shootings, and "freak accidental deaths" daily. But we must remember that these stories are the exceptions––not the rule. In general, we can keep our children safe by following a few guidelines:

❏ *Be aware of the places your children go.*

❏ *Participate in community plans and decisions that place the welfare of children as a priority.*

❏ *Ensure that your children are informed, know to ask questions, and feel comfortable enough to communicate openly with adults.*

❏ *Employ parenting skills that build self-esteem in your children––those who have high self-esteem are usually less easily manipulated or victimized.*

❏ *Arrange for your child to be in programs that provide positive guidance and appropriate supervision at all times.*

❑*Remember that the parenting process is very likely the most important activity in determining the future of a society.*

By becoming a participating advocate for a community that places a high priority on children and in turn fully using community resources to support that position, we as parents can greatly enhance the futures of our children.

Boxes 13-3 to 13-6 offer check lists of information that you should know.

Box 13-3. Check List of What Children Need to Know How to Do

- ❑ To be safe
- ❑ To protect their own bodies
- ❑ To say, "NO"
- ❑ To get help against bullies
- ❑ To tell
- ❑ To be believed
- ❑ To not keep secrets
- ❑ To not accept bribes
- ❑ To refuse touches
- ❑ To never play in deserted or dark places
- ❑ To not talk to strangers
- ❑ To break rules to protect themselves
- ❑ To always walk in a confident manner
- ❑ To trust their own judgment if things don't seem right

Box 13-4. Check List for What Parents Need to Know How to Do

❑ To listen to children

❑ To give children the power of information

❑ To recognize from behavioral indicators when children have problems and need help

❑ To find community resources to help their children when it is needed

❑ To supervise their children at all times

❑ To believe their children—they rarely lie about abuse of any type

❑ To discuss all topics of personal safety in a matter-of-fact way

❑ To choose appropriate caregivers for their child

❑ To build their child's self-esteem with lots of love, praise, and attention

Box 13-5. Check List for Teaching Young Children About Personal Safety Skills

❑ Teach them to tell you if anyone asks them to keep a kiss, hug, or touch a secret. Explain that no one should ask them to do this and you will never be angry at them if they tell you. Ensure that they know they must do this even if it feels good or if someone threatens them.

❑ Explain that it is alright to say NO, if they feel it is safe to do so. Practice with them. Shout NO loudly together. Also, allow them to choose to not hug (or kiss) Great Aunt Mary or Uncle Joe when they come to visit if they don't want to.

❑ Help them understand that their bodies belong to them. Explain that this means their entire body, including their genitals. It is best if children know the correct names for all their body parts. However, if this makes you feel uncomfortable, you can say, "That includes the parts covered by bathing suits." Children who have been abused sometimes have bad or wrong ideas about their bodies: they need to learn to love themselves and be proud of their bodies.

❑ Explain that they don't always have to listen to and obey adults and that you will support them if they feel unsafe.

❑ Tell them they can run away from someone who frightens them.

❑ Help them understand that hugs and kisses are nice but are never kept secret.

> **Box 13-6. Check List for Teaching Older Children and Teens About Personal Safety Skills**
>
> ❏ Talk to them about trusting their intuition. If they have the feeling things are not right, they should leave or get help.
>
> ❏ Help them to establish their own personal limits and give suggestions about getting out of situations or telling others what their limits are.
>
> ❏ Give specific clues about watching out for inappropriate behavior. If, for example, a person makes sexual comments, rubs against them, or is offensive, tell them to excuse themselves, go to another room or the bathroom, telephone someone, or take a taxi home. (If they have no money, tell them you'll pay at the other end.)
>
> ❏ Help them establish a list of people they could go talk to or go to for help. This may or may not include you. There are some things teens would rather not talk to parents about. Tell them that if they go to one of these adults for help, they will be believed and supported. Remember—children, even teens, very rarely lie about sexual assault.
>
> ❏ Suggest taking a course in self-defense or assertiveness to help build their confidence. Make sure that the course is properly run by a qualified person.

RESOURCES FOR PARENTS

Faber, A., & Mazlish, E. (1986) *How to Talk so Kids Will Listen and Listen so Kids Will Talk.* St Paul, MN.: Readleaf Press.

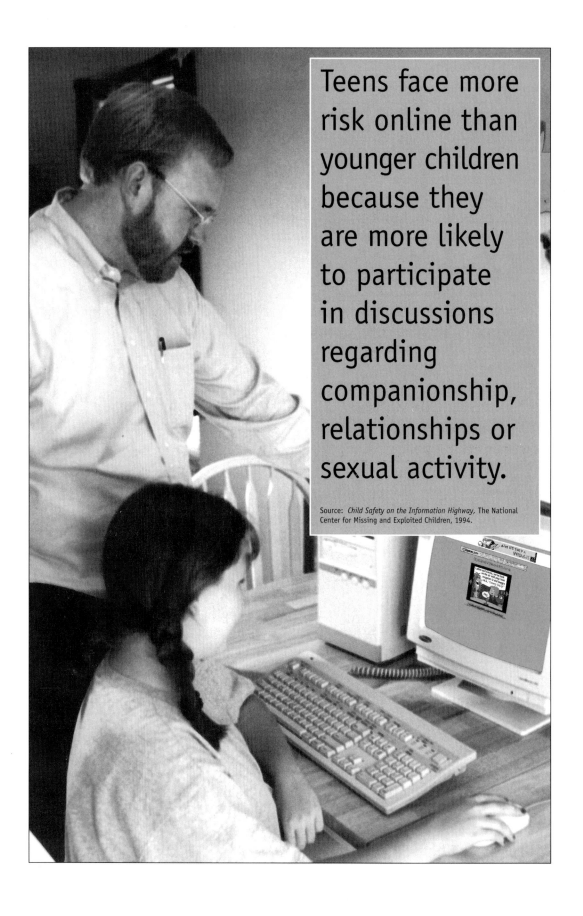

Teens face more risk online than younger children because they are more likely to participate in discussions regarding companionship, relationships or sexual activity.

Source: *Child Safety on the Information Highway,* The National Center for Missing and Exploited Children, 1994.

KEEPING CHILDREN SAFE ON THE INTERNET

DET. MICHAEL SULLIVAN   BECKY J. POWERS
DET. JOE BOVA CONTI   AGENT SCOTT SKINNER, F.B.I.

Every day on the Internet, corrupt individuals are trying to reach children. The following case will give you an idea how your child could be entrapped even while in the safety of his/her own home.

A mother and father notified their local police after their children, who often access the Internet via their home computer, reported coming across a very aggressive person offering sexually explicit information online. Local, state and federal authorities cooperated to bring this person to justice.

During the effort, a female detective went online, posing as a 13-year-old girl named Wendy. She began "chat" sessions with the individual and received graphic images and video files of children engaged in sexual activity. The following, taken from a police report, is a sample of their actual online "conversation."

<Wendy>	*I am going to my aunt's a week from Friday.*
<Caller>	*Really.*
<Caller>	*How long will you be there?*
<Wendy>	*Friday and Saturday leaving late Sunday night.*
<Wendy>	*My parents are going to Chicago.*
<Caller>	*Do you want me to come up and see you?*
<Wendy>	*My aunt works a double shift on the weekend.*
<Caller>	*Who is at the house when she is working, your uncle?*
<Wendy>	*No one. She is single.*
<Caller>	*I can be there at 3 on Friday.*

The online caller then said he wanted to talk with her over the telephone and asked for her telephone number, which "Wendy" gave him. Later, while on the telephone, he asked to meet her and offered her gifts. With detectives listening to the call and approving the meeting, "Wendy" set up a time and place. On the appointed day, the online caller showed up and was arrested.

The online caller turned out to be a married man, with four young children. He worked for a municipal department of recreation as a volunteer coach for children's sports.

In reality, "Wendy" represents any child who uses the Internet and illustrates the need for common sense parental rules governing a child's use of this medium.

WHAT IS THE INTERNET?

We have passed from the Industrial Age into the Information Age—microchips, tiny as they are, have revolutionized our lives and made our society truly global. Children today have never known life without computers and they face an increasingly techno-driven world of the future. Although many families have not yet or may not ever purchase a personal home computer, children still have access to computers at school, where they are both a part of the curriculum and a teaching aid, and at public libraries, where they are indispensable research tools. For a young person growing up in today's world, being without computer skills is akin to being illiterate.

The Internet, too, is rapidly becoming a part of everyone's daily life. As the name implies, the Internet refers to a huge network of computers which are electronically linked via phone and cable lines and satellites so that the users can communicate and access information while "online." The Internet began as a defense project in the 1960s. When universities discovered how useful the Internet would be to share research and advance knowledge, they became involved. Public and corporate America soon followed. Today, anyone can access the Internet provided they have a modem; the right software, known as a "web browser," and a connection point, such as an online service or Internet service provider (ISP). About 30 million people around the globe now go "online."

The World Wide Web (or WWW) is a small part of the total Internet. But it's the part usually accessed because of its sensory appeal. Sites on the web can contain not only colorful graphics, but audio and video clips as well. You can listen to music, see a historical tape, find out what's new at a museum or library, look at art, "talk" via the keyboard to people with similar interests or hobbies, catch the news, take a tour of the White House and do countless other worthwhile activities.

No matter what age groups your children fall into, the Internet has something for them. For very young children, the Internet offers learning games, clubs and publications. For teens, there are chat groups, online magazines called cyberzines, games and teen clubs. Students can access organization and government sites, academic resources, virtual exploration sites and commercial education sites.

The Internet runs the gamut of human knowledge and is updated more frequently than any printed material ever could be. Children and teens can benefit greatly from the self-directed learning experiences which the Internet provides and especially from the boost in confidence that comes when they have successfully navigated the 'Net to find a particularly obscure fact.

So while it's true that the Internet and computers have their dangers, the benefits of their usage far outweigh the risks. To bar access to computers is unrealistic and would be like asking teenagers not to drive because accidents sometimes happen. As with all other technological advances, such as the car or TV, parents need to look for creative, common sense solutions to protect children.

> **"To bar access to computers is unrealistic . . . parents need to look for creative, common sense solutions to protect children."**

KNOWING THE 'NET

The best solution to protect children as they use the Internet is for parents to guide and monitor, just as they guided and monitored all of their children's efforts to grow and mature. Parents need to sit down with their children at the computer and "surf the 'Net," or sample the variety of sites and services available online. It may be that your children know more than you do about computers; if so, let them teach you about the Internet and experience a growing sense of self-esteem that comes from playing the role of teacher. Together, you'll find sites you both enjoy visiting and talking about. Opening the lines of communication between you and your children is essential to protecting them online and in all other areas of their lives.

Before we can address safety concerns, we need to define the areas we'll be talking about. **Box 1** explains the various kinds of online structures.

WHAT ARE THE RISKS ASSOCIATED WITH USING THE INTERNET?

Some of the 30 million people accessing the Internet will do so for inappropriate or illegal reasons. Some will construct web sites containing adult or pornographic material. Others will use the chat rooms and bulletin boards to talk with a child, gain his or her confidence and personal information and arrange a face-to-face meeting. They may even put together a site which has the allure of a commercial enterprise and use a "marketing survey" to gain information about a child. While young children most often stumble upon adult or pornographic web sites, teenagers often are trapped via their participation in online discussions, where they may freely discuss relationships and sexual activities.

The Internet offers an anonymity impossible to achieve with any other form of communication. This anonymity sometimes frees people to speak much more intimately over the Internet than they ever would in person. It also allows people to adopt a disguise when communicating over the Internet. **If your child tells you he knows an Internet friend very well, remind him that all he knows is what this friend has told him. None of it may be the truth.**

You may wonder how a child could easily find inappropriate Web sites. Most children learn how to use a search engine in school. Put yourself in the

---

Box 1. Online Structures Which You Will Encounter

Address—the location of a site on the Internet which holds specific information or is the mailbox of an E-mail user.

Bulletin boards (BBS)—sites operated by individuals, businesses or organizations for the electronic "posting" of messages, usually regarding a particular theme or interest. Many BBSs feature adult material and most attempt to block minors from accessing that material.

Chat room—a location in an online service which, when accessed, allows users to "talk" to one another by typing messages on their keyboards. Each user's message is shown onscreen in real time and can be read by any other user in the "room."

E-mail (Electronic mail)—a message sent from one computer to another, via a modem and telephone or cable lines.

Home page—the entry point to a web site for an individual, group, organization or business.

Internet—the largest of all computer networks, the Internet is completely unregulated and without any monitors or controls. Information of every type imaginable is available somewhere on the Internet.

Modem—a special phone which enables your computer to connect, via the phone lines, with the Internet. If your system has a modem, it is probably installed inside the computer.

Online services—commercial businesses which provide connections to the Internet, as well as content ranging from shopping opportunities and games to business news and health information. These services often screen content and provide parental controls.

Search engine—an online research tool. By specifying a topic, you can view a list of sites related to that topic and access the sites you want to see. Search engines can be used to locate adult material.

Web browser—a software program which enables your computer to receive text and images from the Internet. Along with a modem and Internet service provider, it is essential for accessing the Internet. You can receive browser software free by joining an online service.

World Wide Web—a portion of the Internet characterized by its colorful, graphic content. Addresses of sites on the Web are preceded by "www."

---

shoes of a 12-year-old boy who wants to see nude photos of girls, but doesn't know the Internet address for these. After entering the Internet, you would access a search engine. Then you would type in the words, "nude girls" and touch the appropriate key to tell the engine to search the Internet for sites with nude girls. With just one search engine, you could access over 98,000 sites—each one containing pictures that can be viewed for free or saved in your computer's memory for later viewing. You could also receive these images via E-mail.

Remember, though, search engines are not the problem When used appropriately, search engines can help a child with school work or hobbies. What's needed is supervised usage or the child's agreement to stick to a set of safety rules when online. You can even check to see where in cyberspace your child has been by looking at the "cache" or "history folder" in your web browser software.

In summary, the risks which your children may encounter online are:

• Exposure to material of a sexual or violent nature

• Direct communication with an individual who is looking for an inappropriate relationship

• Harassing, hostile or otherwise rude E-mail or BBS messages

How Parents Can Reduce the Risks Their Children Face

Parents shouldn't feel powerless simply because the Internet is a complex medium with which their children may have more experience than they do. As with any other life experience their children encounter, parents can exercise a great deal of authority simply by becoming involved. Showing an interest in and carefully monitoring a child's activity on the Internet will be more successful in terms of protection than forbidding its usage outright, which will only make it more attractive to a curious youngster.

Steps Parents Can Take to Protect their Children

Let your children know you're interested in their online activities

• Don't let their desire for privacy overtake their need for parental supervision. Ask your children to show you where they go online and stay in touch during their online sessions.

• Use the Internet yourself and become familiar with the online services your children access.

- Read up on the subject or talk about your concerns with other parents.

Set up guidelines for online usage

Children feel more secure when their activities, including computer usage, are governed by clearcut rules, definite boundaries and sure consequences. For instance, you may want to specify the type of sites they can visit and the amount of time they can spend online, especially for fun, rather than school-related, activities. For a teenager, you may want to curb late-night usage, especially of chat rooms and bulletin boards. Gather input from your children, decide on the acceptable sites and times and then post this information near the computer as a reminder.

Emphasize that online exploration is something for the whole family. Just as it is unwise to put a TV with access to adults-only channels in your child's room, you should not allow a computer with access to adult sites and chat rooms to be placed out of your sight in your child's room. Instead, locate the computer in the family room so that everyone can be involved and monitoring is easier. You'll be able to get to know your children's online friends just as you know their friends from school.

Make sure your child understands that a stranger is a stranger. Just because the conversation takes place over the computer does not change that fact. Your child knows that he or she shouldn't speak with a stranger on the playground, and the same rules should apply to computer conversations. Children need to be told that even giving out just a bit of personal information can allow a stranger to find out where they live. Currently, there are search engines that allow anyone to put in a telephone number and receive the name and address for that number. The programs work only for listed phone numbers. These programs also link to neighborhood maps, supplying a stranger—possibly a pedophile—with the exact directions to your house.

Never allow your child to meet someone in person whom he or she knows only from online conversations unless you are present. If an online relationship grows to the point where your child and the other person want to meet, you should know about it. The place for the meeting should be a public place, and if the other person is a child, he or she should also bring parents. In this way, everyone can feel safe and have the freedom to simply walk away. Generally, if all the other person is interested in is making a friend, having a chaperone present shouldn't be a problem.

Don't allow your children to send pictures of themselves online without your permission. You never know what another person will do with a picture. With very little knowledge and a basic graphics program, any image can be altered, or "morphed," and it would be nearly impossible to tell. Angry ex-husbands have been known to morph the face of their ex-wife onto the nude image of an adult film personality and then post it on the Internet or mail it to neighbors. The same thing could happen to any image your child sends over the Internet.

Here is a sample list of rules which you can discuss with your children and post near the computer:

- Never reveal your password to anyone online, not even to online service staff members.

- Never reveal identifying information—real names (first or last), family member names, home addresses, details of parent's work, school or team names, telephone numbers, social security numbers or credit card numbers in a chat room or in a bulletin board message. And never give out this information via E-mail to someone whom you don't know. Remember: No matter how friendly someone seems on the Internet, that person is a stranger. He may even be an adult pretending to be a child.

- Never accept offers of merchandise or information or give out your street address for deliveries without getting your parent's permission.

- Never send a photo of yourself or offer a physical description of yourself or family members over the Internet.

- Never continue a conversation that makes you feel uncomfortable or becomes personal. Just "hang up" on the conversation by going to another area of the Internet. Tell your parents what happened.

- Never answer E-mail or BBS items which are suggestive, obscene, rude or make you feel uncomfortable in any way. Tell your parents if you come across such messages and forward the messages to the service provider. Remember: It isn't your fault if you get such a message. You've done nothing to deserve getting a message like that.

- Never arrange to meet someone in person whom you've met online. If your parents do agree to a meeting, make sure you arrange it for a public spot and take a parent along.

- Be careful when responding to E-mail. Return addresses can be falsified to make the message look innocent. If you can't verify who it came from, don't answer it.

Why chat rooms can be very dangerous for your children

Children's most popular area of the Internet—and the most dangerous—is the chat room. Chat rooms allow users of the Internet to converse with other users in a real-time format no matter where in the world they are located. Because of the nature of the Internet, a local telephone call to your service provider allows you to travel virtually anywhere in the world and converse, by typing messages on the keyboard, with total strangers.

Some of the most frequently used chat rooms exist on Internet Relay Chat (IRC) or within the databases of Internet service providers, such as America Online (AOL). These chat rooms are listed by name, which usually gives an idea of the topic the room is discussing. To participate, your child selects a screen name—much like a "handle"—by which he or she will be known while chatting. There is no verification that the name chosen reflects who the person really is. Someone could use a name that would indicate he was a 12-year-old girl when in fact he is a 35-year-old man.

After selecting a room, your child's screen name appears in the room. Most chat formats allow for a brief description or profile of the users. In this area, basic information about the user is stored for viewing by other users. Once your child enters the room, others can check this profile. A pedophile can learn how old your child is and whether this is a boy or girl. He may also learn where your child lives and the school he attends.

What could a pedophile do in these chat rooms? Some may enter a room and "lurk" (be in the room watching the conversation taking place but not participating). This way, he can observe your child's likes and dislikes; relationship factors, such as if your child recently had an argument with you and whether or not others in the room are friendly with your child.

These are not new behaviors for pedophiles. Before the Internet, a pedophile wanting to meet children went to the playground or schoolyard and watched the children there. This had a certain risk associated with it—that of possibly being seen by teachers, school workers or mothers keeping watch over their children. Now the pedophile can visit the "virtual park" and speak directly with children from the privacy of their own homes without fear of detection by mothers, teachers or watchful neighbors. If the pedophile feels even the least bit concerned about being discovered talking to a child, he can break off the contact and disappear into the anonymity of the Internet.

When the pedophile begins a conversation in a chat room with your child, it starts off innocently because everyone else in the room can see the messages. However, after a brief period of time, he may suggest a private forum for the conversation. Most chat programs allow for a private method of chatting between two people. At this point, the pedophile will try to find out how safe it is to speak with your child by asking questions such as:

- Are you home alone?

- Who else uses the computer?

- Where is the computer located?

The pedophile will generally end the conversation if your child replies that she is not alone and others use the computer, which is located in the family room. But if your child tells the pedophile that he is home alone, the computer is in his room and it is only for his use, the pedophile may move the conversation to the next level. Through a series of questions, that pedophile will gain your child's trust and attempt to make it seem as though they can trust only each other and no one else.

What does the pedophile talk about once this level is reached? Generally, the pedophile first sends jokes that are off color or suggestive to gauge your child's reaction. From this, he may move into a conversation about sexual experience, with the goal of lowering your child's inhibitions. As the conversation continues, the pedophile may describe sexual techniques or positions and may ask your child to attempt masturbation. To show your child that this is a normal practice and that "everyone does it," the pedophile may send computer-produced images showing other people involved in the activity.

After the photos have been sent, the pedophile may try to increase the amount of trust between him and your child by asking that he or she delete the pictures, saying that he would be in a lot of trouble if anyone else saw these pictures. The pedophile may tell your child that he is trusting him or her to keep this activity private—asking your child to promise never to tell anyone about these conversations and promising to keep it secret as well. As these types of conversations continue and the trust level increases, the pedophile will ask for a meeting in person.

What to do if your teen enjoys taking risks online

The anonymity of the Internet, which protects teens who are online, also leads them to do dangerous things. Thinking they are untouchable, some teens will deliberately engage people online whom they call "creeps" or "perverts." Pushing discussions into inappropriate zones and even setting up meetings are part of the risk-taking behavior.

If your teenagers are engaging in risk-taking, make it clear to them how important it is that they stop. This is not an issue of trust, but one of safety. Their actions are unsafe and must cease.

What to do if you come across illegal material online

The National Center for Missing and Exploited Children wants to be alerted to the presence of any illegal material online, such as child pornography, threatening messages or evidence of criminal action. You can report such sites to the Center by calling 1-800-843-5678. You should also notify your online service.

What technology offers to keep your children safe

Several technological innovations will help you keep your children safe while using the Internet.

Online services often have a Parental Control Center which will allow you, at no additional cost, to block chat rooms, forums and member meeting rooms, instant messages (real-time messages viewed only by the sender and receiver), bulletin board services and news groups.

Logs, which allow you to note where on the service your children are spending their time, are offered by many online services. The services may also let you set up a children's account which allows access only to specific services. By following the suggestions of the Parental Control Center, you'll be setting up the service as a resource, not as an interactive experience. Such a setup carries the least risk and most value for children. **Remember, however, that these controls are not foolproof and that children often are able to get around them.**

Your online service will also help you choose a screen name and E-mail address which is unrelated to your real name to give you and your children some privacy when conversing online.

Software programs have also been developed to help parents protect children. Some programs rate web site content, similar to movie ratings. Programs such as *Net Nanny, SurfWatch, CyberSitter, CyberPatrol* or *Internet Filter* prevent your children from entering sites dealing with subjects you specify and block certain files from being sent to your children. Some of the programs prevent users from entering personal information into web site forms. Others restrict the child's ability to send or read E-mail. Generally, parents can configure the program to block only the sites which they consider objectionable.

Filter and blocking programs are useful only to a point. Not all software programs, for instance, would red flag a pornography file with an address of "history." On the other hand, a perfectly legitimate online file, such as NASA's Mars exploration photos, which is listed online with an address of "Marsex," would be blocked because the address contains the word "sex." The bottom line is, software programs or any technology were never meant to replace parental supervision.

Ultimately, just like all of the other hazards our children face—drugs, alcohol, peer pressure and violence—the best way to deal with the subject is to talk to your children. Tell them that you understand what can happen and that sometimes the items sent to the computer are not their fault. However, make sure that they understand that they must tell you about (1) anything that is sent that is inappropriate and (2) anyone who asks them for personal information. Open communication between you and your child is the best form of parental control.

Internet Safety Tips—A Checklist for Parents

❑ Instruct your children not to give out personal information online such as their password, full name, address, telephone number, age, gender, school name, sports team name, credit card information, or social security number.

❑ Talk to your children often about what they are doing online. There is no substitute for parental supervision. Be aware of what type of activity your child is involved in online.

❑ Provide your child with clear, simple instructions about how to avoid danger and what to do if something happens.

❑ Set safety rules that are appropriate for your child's age that both you and your child understand and agree to and then post these by the computer.

❑ Limit the amount of time your child spends online. Late-night times and excessive use of the computer by an adolescent may signal a problem.

❑ Make the online experience a family activity. Set up the computer in a central area of the home, such as the family room or living room and use it to plan vacations, purchase books, listen to music, preview videos, or help with research on school assignments with your children.

❑ Use online experiences as another way to teach responsibility, good conduct, and values.

❑ Use common sense when online. Remember that everything you read online may not be the truth and any offer that is too good to be true probably is not true.

Questions That May Be Asked by a Pedophile to Gain the Confidence and Trust of a Child

NOTE: Pedophiles also empathize with the child, especially if the child is feeling emotionally down.

How are you?

What are your favorite things?

How old are you?

Where are you now? (Verifying location of computer.)

Where are your parents?

What school do you go to?

What is your favorite class?

What time do you get home from school?

Do your parents work?

Do you have brothers or sisters?

Do you play any sports?
    Which ones are your favorites?

Do you like music?
    What are your favorite groups/singers?

What are your favorite foods?

Would you like to see some pictures?

Can you send me your picture?

Would you like to get together?

REMEMBER: Not all conversations that might contain these questions are cause for alarm. Conversations between your child and someone else in an online chat room can be an honest exchange of information that can further a friendship.

SUGGESTED READINGS

Abduction Avoidance, Awareness and Self Defense. Online at www.umakarate.com

Child Safety Tips, 1998, the Polly Klaas Foundation, P.O. Box 800, Petaluma, CA 94953. (800) 587-HELP. www.pollyklaas.org/safety.htm

Censorship/Freedom of Speech: *Child Safety on the Internet.* www.voicenet.com/~cranmer/censorship.html

The Children's Partnership. *The Parent's Guide to the Information Superhighway.* Online. September 1996. Online at www.childrenspartnership.org

Dial, D.E.: *Safety Tips for Parents and Children on the Internet,* 1998, available from the Naperville Police Department, 1350 Aurora Ave., Naperville, IL 60540.

The Internet and our Children, NetNanny Software International, Inc. www.netnanny.com

Kraizer, S.: *The Safe Child Book: A Common Sense Approach to Protecting Children and Teaching Children to Protect Themselves,* New York, 1996, Fireside Books/A Simon & Schuster Trade Paperback Original. (Also online at http://safechild.org/Book.htm)

Magid, Lawrence J.: *Child Safety on the Information Highway.* Arlington (VA): National Center for Missing and Exploited Children; 1996. Also online at www.larrysworld.com

Safe Child Program. *Safety on the Internet.* www.safechild.org

Safety Tips for Kids on the Internet, Federal Bureau of Investigation Educational Web Publication. Online at www.fbi.gov/kids/internet/internet.htm

US Department of Education. *Parents Guide to the Internet.* Online. 1997; online at www.ed.gov/pubs/parents/internet/

INDEX

R

Rash, diaper, neglect and, 15

Rayner, Claire, 188

References for caregivers, 123

Regressed child molesters, 48, 49

Regressive behavior, 37

Reinforcement

 negative, 5-6

 positive; *see* Positive reinforcement

Relevant information, collecting, caregivers and, 111-114

Restlessness, 35

Risk, the Internet and 202

 how parents can reduce 203-208

Rules and expectations, parenting styles and, 6-7

Running away, 41

S

Sadism, 50

Safety

 personal, skills of, 77-82, 187, 188, 189, 194, 195

 in prevention of abuse, 189

SAM team; *see* Special Assessment and Management team

"Schematic" drawings, art therapy and, 165

Schmitt, Barton D., 8

School performance, change in, 38

Screening caregivers, 111-114, 123, 190-191

Search engines, Internet and 199-211

Secrets, 82

Seduction, 49-50

Self-portraits, art therapy and, 150

Sexual abuse, 45-54

 definition of, 45, 46-47, 75

 dynamics of, 75-76

 how to respond to child's report of, 50-52

 prevention of, 185-187

 ramifications of, 129-132

 reasons that children do not disclose, 76

signs of, 52-53, 140-149, 152-156

 what to do if you suspect your child may have been a victim of, 82-85

 what to do if your child is a victim of, 85-86

Sexual Abuse team; *see* Special Assessment and Management team

Sexual "acting out," 33-35

Sexual assault, 46

Sexual exploitation, 47

Sexualized behavior, 83

Sexually indiscriminate child molester, 49

Shaken infant syndrome, 22-24

Shelter, inadequate, neglect and, 58, 59

Sibling, adjusting to, art therapy and, 169

Sides of body, injuries to, 13

SIDS; *see* Sudden infant death syndrome

Skin injuries, 15-16

Sleep disturbances, 35

Sleeping arrangements, inadequate, neglect and, 59

SMART team, 188

Society's commitment to children, 179-187

Software programs, Internet and, 205

Spanking

 in caregiver programs, 120

 guidelines for, 8-9

Special Assessment and Management (SAM; Sexual Abuse) team, 31, 39

Specific behavioral indicators of abuse, 31, 32, 33-35

Stepparent, adjusting to, art therapy and, 170-171

Stocking-glove burns, 22

Stress causing behavioral change, 32

Structural hazards, neglect and, 60

Substance abuse, 25-26, 41, 61, 67, 182

Sudden infant death syndrome (SIDS), 19

Suffocation, 19, 57

Suggestions, alteration of child's stories by, 52

Suicide attempts, 40

Supervision

 by caregivers, 192

 neglect and, 62

G. W. Medical Publishing, Inc.

2601 METRO BOULEVARD • SAINT LOUIS, MISSOURI 63043-2411
ph 1-800-600-0330 • 314-298-0330 • fax 314-298-2820
www.gwmedical.com

Nearly 1,000 photos—more than 1,000 pages... on virtually all apects of child abuse

TWO-VOLUME SET—NEW SECOND EDITION

CHILD MALTREATMENT

James A. Monteleone, M.D.

$195.00 *plus shipping and handling.* ISBN 1-878060-26-0

*The world's only encyclopedia of child abuse—
the most comprehensive set of books available!*

- **More than 225 new photographs and 250 new pages**
- **Every chapter revised to include latest research and statistical data**
- **Authored by a nationally recognized expert with seasoned clinicians contributing**

From bruises and burns to sexual abuse and on to neglect and abandonment, each of the volume's 28 chapters covers in explicit detail the essential diagnosing criteria; the demographics of at-risk children; incidence statistics; possible nonabuse etiology; conducting the examination and interview; suggested diagnostic studies, including laboratory and radiology work; evaluation of findings and sample case histories. In-depth analysis of proffered histories shows you how to separate truth from lies.

You'll find the chapters on sexual abuse definitive and invaluable—they will become your preferred source for information on age-appropriate interview techniques, step-by-step examinations, analysis of genital findings and documentation.

The medical professional, social worker or law enforcer will find these references a must for information on reporting statutes, child protective services, investigation procedures, litigation, evidence review, analysis of defenses and elements of testimony.

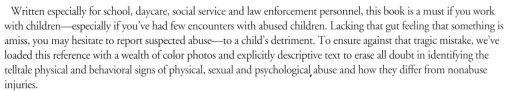

G. W. Medical Publishing, Inc.

2601 METRO BOULEVARD • SAINT LOUIS, MISSOURI 63043-2411
ph 1-800-600-0330 • 314-298-0330 • fax 314-298-2820
www.gwmedical.com

Order Form

Copy and mail to: G.W. Medical Publishing, 2601 Metro Blvd., St. Louis, MO 63043
Ph 314-298-0330 • Fax 314-298-2820 • www.gwmedical.com
e-mail: info@gwmedical.com

Yes, I'd like to order the following books. I understand that if I am not satisfied with the books, I can return them within 30 days for a complete refund.

_____ **Child Maltreatment,** 2nd Ed., 2-vol. set $195.00* (ISBN: 1-878060-26-0). Pub 1/98.

_____ **Recognition of Child Abuse for the Mandated Reporter,** 2nd Ed., $39.95* (ISBN: 1-878060-24-4). Pub 9/96.

_____ **Child Abuse Quick Reference for Healthcare Professionals, Social Services and Law Enforcement,** $39.95* (ISBN: 1-878060-28-7). Pub 1/98.

*Order additional copies of **A Parent's & Teacher's Handbook** below!*

_____ **A Parent's & Teacher's Handbook on Identifying and Preventing Child Abuse,** $19.95* (ISBN: 1-878060-27-9). Pub 7/98.

Please check payment option:

❑ Check enclosed.   Bill my credit card: ❑ Mastercard   ❑ VISA   ❑ American Express

Acct. No. _____   Exp. Date _____

Signature _____

Bill me with my Purchase Order* _____

Shipping information:

Name _____

Institution _____

Address _____

Dept./Mail Stop _____

City _____ State _____ Zip _____

Phone (_____)_____ Fax (_____)_____

* All orders are billed for postage, handling, and state sales tax where applicable. All prices subject to change without notice. If using a purchase order, please attach it to this form. Money-back Guarantee: If you are not 100% satisfied, simply return the book(s). Your money will be promptly refunded.